Volunteering

101 Ways You
Can Improve the World
and Your Life

Douglas M. Lawson, Ph.D.

A L
T I
PUBLISHING

20% of the publisher's receipts from the sale of this book will be contributed to charity by the author and ALTI Publishing. To learn how your nonprofit organization may benefit from this donation or how ALTI may create a tailor-made book for you, call (800) 284-8537.

ISBN 1-883051-17-7

Printed in the United States of America
10 9 8 7 6 5 4 3 2 1

Design: White Light Publishing
Cover: George Foster
Copyediting: Sherri Schottlaender

Quantity discounts and special editions are available.
For information, please contact:
ALTI Publishing
P.O. Box 28025
San Diego, CA 92198
Phone: (800) 284-8537
Fax: (619) 485-9878
E-mail: whilbig@altipublishing.com

Distributed to the trade by National Book Network (800) 462-6420

 Printed on Recycled Paper

Dedication

This book is dedicated to three volunteers who changed the world and whose lives were taken from us the same week: PRINCESS DIANA, VICTOR FRANKL, and MOTHER TERESA; one a Protestant, one a Jew, and one a Catholic.

I remember when I used to sit on hospital beds and hold people's hands, people used to be sort of shocked because they'd never seen this before. To me, it was quite normal.

— PRINCESS DIANA

We who lived in the concentration camps can remember those who walked through the huts comforting others, giving away their last piece of bread. They may have been few in number, but they offer sufficient proof that every thing can be taken from a human being but one thing — the last of our freedoms — to choose our spirit in any given set of circumstances.

— VICTOR FRANKL

In this world, we cannot do great things. We can only do small things with great love.

— MOTHER TERESA

Introduction

Every year millions of Americans volunteer at more than one million nonprofit organizations throughout the United States. These volunteers make it possible for these agencies to serve people in need in this country and throughout the world. From its early pioneer days, American has built its strong foundation upon volunteer support. This has been true from the "barn-raising" days of the early pioneers to the "fund-raising" and "friend-raising" era in which we now live. As we prepare to enter the twenty-first century, Americans continue to volunteer to make the world a better place in which to live, and many are finding it is not what you get that makes for happiness in life, it's what you give away.

General Colin Powell continues to lead this nation as Chairman of the Presidents' Summit for America's Future. This historic summit was established to be a celebration of our nation's heritage of volunteer citizen service and a call to action to turn the tide of America's fifteen million disadvantaged youth by the end of the century by organizing volunteers in more than one hundred communities and fifty states throughout this country. General Powell addressed the Presidents' Summit in April 1997: "All of us can spare thirty minutes a week or an hour a week. All of us can give an extra dollar. All of us can touch someone who doesn't look like us, who doesn't speak like us, who may not dress like us but, by God, needs us in their lives. . . . And so let us all join in this great crusade."

Americans are also being encouraged to volunteer by Oprah Winfrey, who is generously lending her name and celebrity status to encourage active volunteerism through a national movement she is calling "Oprah's Angel Network." Oprah has used her popular television show to deliver her specific five-point program for volunteer participation in activities around the country: 1)by asking Americans to save their spare change to deposit into the world's largest piggy bank for college scholarships and needy youth; 2) by joining other volunteers with Habitat for Humanity International to build 205 homes by the end of the year in every town that broadcasts Oprah; 3) by asking people to work free of charge once a week or once a month by using their job-related skills and talents to help someone in need; 4) by helping at a child's school by teaching a child to read, or other projects; 5) and, by doing mini-miracles in their communities by using their time and talent in acts of kindness that make a difference in the world.

Ted Turner is challenging all the millionaires and billionaires of the world to give back to others that which they really do not need themselves. He issued this challenge with his dramatic announcement in 1997 that over the next ten years he would give $1 billion to the United Nations Association to help people in need.

George Soros, a European-born American philanthropist and financier, has announced he will donate $500 million over the next three years to Russia to aid them in improving their health care system, retraining their military personnel for civilian jobs, and improving their educational system. Mr. Soros has donated more than $350 million a year since 1994 to his foundations in more than thirty countries.

There are also generous heroes from the corporate world. Wal-Mart, the world's largest retail corporation, has earned an excellent reputation for community service by voluntarily giving back to the communities they serve. They have raised and contributed more than $52 million in support of the United Way agencies and more than $60 million for the Miracle Children's Network. They have also awarded $11 million in college scholarships and pledged $1 million to the United Negro College Fund. Wal-Mart has certainly set an outstanding example of voluntary generosity for other corporations to follow.

This book was written for today's volunteer who is already responding to General Powell's call to action, "Oprah's Angel Network," and Ted Turner's challenge. But more importantly, it was also written for those who have not yet experienced the joy of volunteering. For those who are active volunteers, the book answers many questions that confront them every day. For the reader who has not yet jumped into the delightful swimming pool of volunteering, the answer to your questions may be found within this book.

Most of us do not know that volunteers live happier, healthier, and longer lives than non-volunteers. I want you to have that knowledge and continue your volunteer swim in the refreshing pool of love for others that life has for you, or begin your volunteering by jumping into the pool today. By the way, the water is wonderful.

I suggest you turn to the contents page of this book and search for questions for which you most need answers. After reading the answers to the volunteer questions that most concern you, I suggest you read a question a day for 101 days. After three months I hope this book will have become an inspiration to you and you will become a volunteer for the rest of your life. Many people you have never met are counting on you to make that positive decision. They need you, but you need to volunteer even more. Your happiness, health, and length of life literally depend on whether you are ready to share your time, talent, and treasure with others. I hope this book will play a small part in your decision to make volunteering a vital part of your life, and in doing so your activities will help to change the world for the better as did the efforts of Princess Diana, Victor Frankl, and Mother Teresa.

Acknowledgments

This book would not have been possible without the excellent writing talent of Phyllis Estes and the editing skills of Theresa Alexander. Phyllis worked tirelessly with me on the concept, format, and first draft. Theresa was my assistant as the finishing touches were put on it. To both of them I owe a debt of gratitude I cannot fully acknowledge.

To the more than one thousand nonprofit clients I have served as a professional fund-raiser over the past thirty-two years I also owe my thanks. They, and the thousands of volunteers who fulfill their missions every day, were the inspiration for this book.

Wayne Hilbig, president of Alti Publishing, was the driving force behind this book's conception. He urged me to write it and he was my champion as the pages finally went to print. Thanks also to Manuel Arango for his example and support in making this book a reality.

Finally, I want to thank the millions of volunteers who every day make it possible for the work of more than one million nonprofit agencies in America to be accomplished. They are the people that keep America strong and they are the individuals who truly inspired the writing of this book.

— Douglas M. Lawson
March, 1998

CONTENTS

SECTION I: Volunteering and You

SECTION II: Volunteering and Life

SECTION III: Volunteering and Others

SECTION IV: Volunteering with Corporations and Charities

SECTION V: Volunteering around the World

Living is the art of loving,
Loving is the art of caring,
Caring is the art of sharing,
Sharing is the art of living.

— ANONYMOUS

SECTION I

Volunteering and You

*It is a rare and high privilege to be in a position
to help people understand the differences
that they can make not only in their own lives
but in the lives of others
by simply giving of themselves.*

— HELEN BOOSALIS

— 1 —

How can I volunteer when I have no time to volunteer?

If you have no time to volunteer then you are missing the greatest gift in life: happiness. Money cannot buy happiness, but giving of yourself to others increases your abilities to generate great emotional rewards. Success cannot buy you health, but helping others has been proven to improve emotional and physical well-being.

It is common these days to see your friends work-work-work until they develop a health crisis, experience the failure of a significant relationship, or suffer a financial setback. Only then do they finally step back from their busy lives to reassess themselves. So often we see these same people pull back from their chaotic lifestyles to spend more time giving to their families, participating in their churches, synagogues, or mosques, or giving time to help with a community issue or charity. Why wait until you face a crisis to evaluate the priorities in your life? Join forces with the millions of other Americans who spend their time volunteering!

The question is not, "Do I have enough time to volunteer?" The real question is "Can I afford not to give time to be a volunteer?" Your happiness, health, relationships, and emotional well-being depend upon your answer.

To be a good volunteer takes faith and then the willingness to act on that faith. We must have faith in people, in ourselves, in the spiritual resources that exist in each person.

— ARTHUR B. LANGLIE

— 2 —

How can I find out where to volunteer?

Most people volunteer within six miles of their own home! You are needed in your own backyard. Finding a volunteer job can be compared to finding a paid job that suits your skills, talents, and the time you have available. Begin your search by determining what areas interest you. There is a volunteer center near you and it is easy to find that center: just call (800) 272-8306 and ask for a copy of the most recent *Volunteer Center Directory*. Or contact Volunteer Net on the Internet at volnet@aol.com, or while waiting for the information from the volunteer center e-mail: SMEvans944@aol.com. Call the local office of United Way, The Salvation Army, The American Red Cross, or Habitat for Humanity International or a similar non-profit agency. Once you open the door to the world of volunteering, you will be directed by competent dedicated people. Suddenly you will find volunteer opportunities everywhere you turn.

Would you like to work with children? At a local university? For a crisis service like suicide prevention or in a volunteer fire department? In health care? With the homeless? Elderly? Those living with cancer? The disabled? Would you like to be involved at a committee level to raise money or would you rather help people directly by teaching literacy, delivering meals to shut-ins, or working in the gift shop of a hospital? Your volunteer choices are virtually endless and easy to locate.

There are some excellent books that will help you find out where to volunteer. Among them are Tracy Daniel Connors' *The Volunteer Management Handbook*, Paul J. Ilsley's *Enhancing the Volunteer Experience*, David C.

Forward's *Heroes After Hours*, Susan J. Ellis's *By the People*, and Marlene Wilson's *You Can Make a Difference!*

America was built on a foundation of volunteerism. Each generation has its chance to make that foundation even stronger. If you want to become a part of that volunteer tradition, you can do so today. Information on how to do this is at your fingertips.

These are indeed grave times, difficult times, complex times, for your institution. But there have never been more opportunities. And there has never been a more exciting time to be a volunteer for a good cause.

— JEROLD PANAS

— 3 —

Why should I volunteer?
What's in it for me?

A longer, healthier, happier life is your reward for volunteering. Giving of yourself offers you opportunities to glimpse life beyond your own unique perspective and find a greater understanding of the world around you by discovering a true sense of compassion for yourself and others. We learn how to live by learning to face the world around us and offering ourselves for service where we can help make a difference.

If all the world stayed home indulging only in personal, individual pursuits, we would be reduced to wild animals who defend their territories with cruel vengeance. However, in contrast, when we open our hearts and leave our homes and go into our communities, we find beauty, mystery, and the true pleasure of connection to the world in which we live. In fact, community involvement actually reduces our level of fear of the unknown because we see the world with open eyes instead of through imaginary fearful thoughts. Facing life by addressing needs in our immediate neighborhood or city teaches us about our own belief system and reveals to us how the world really works. When we learn about the real world we are capable of listening to the truth told by other people, and then life becomes a harmony.

The busy "marketplace" of life has produced a culture of people directed toward individualistic pursuits. In contrast, it has also produced a culture of givers who are willing to step outside their personal needs long enough to find a deeper, richer significance in their lives that money, fame, beauty, or education cannot buy. The pearl of great price is service to others. The only way to find your life is to lose it first in service to others. And that's what we really want, a life full of meaning. That's what volunteering is all about. Why not start today? You have nothing to gain but a better life, something you have always wanted and deserved.

***Wealth, position, fame, and even elusive
happiness will be mine, eventually,
if I determine to render more and
better service, each day,
than I am being paid to render.***

— OG MANDINO

What can I possibly do?
I don't feel I have any talents.

Volunteering provides opportunities to develop new talents by working with trained teams on specific goals. Many people have turned those new skills into viable paying jobs. Many find their volunteer network invaluable in locating jobs and new friends. A degree of self-analysis is required to find certain areas that pique your interest so that a volunteering job will be a good match for your personality and curiosity. Top agencies offer training to help ensure your success as a volunteer by offering small group lectures or mentors until you're comfortable enough to try your wings.

Call your local volunteer center or mayor's office and ask them if they can recommend any agencies offering training for the development of new skills in areas that interest you. But the best training comes from following the footwear manufacturer's advertising: "Just Do It." Does it take talent to serve soup to the hungry? No — just do it. Does it take talent to visit an older adult in a nursing home? No — just do it. It doesn't take talent to volunteer. It just takes you, and it takes you just the way you are.

Everybody can be great
because anybody can serve.
You don't have to have a college degree to serve.
You don't have to make your subject
and verbs agree to serve.
You only need a heart full of grace,
a soul generated by love.

— Martin Luther King Jr.

How can I volunteer
when I don't have any money?

You don't need to have any money to volunteer. All you need is a willing heart and a desire to give to others. There is a magic and mystery about volunteering. The volunteer with no money gets back more than he or she ever gives.

Charities and social service agencies would be happy to have you offer your time rather than your money to further their cause. In helping others, you will find your self-esteem is greatly enhanced; you will have more energy and a higher morale, which makes you an attractive commodity for better employment. Giving of yourself is the key ingredient to finding a new direction for your life.

It is ironic that in life the very things we need to survive (money, for example) often become a part of our life when we are concentrating our energies in a different direction. Volunteering does not require money, it only needs your time and talent. But in the giving of your time and talent to others, you open yourself to the possible blessings of new monetary rewards gained through meeting exciting people who are also serving others.

The be-all and end-all of life should not be
to get rich, but to enrich the world.

B. C. FORBES

— 6 —

How can volunteering enhance my dating life?

How can I find Mr. Wonderful? Where is Ms. Fabulous of my dreams? Are they really at the local pick-up bar? Can I actually meet them at the health club? Perhaps — but probably not. Mr. Wonderful and Ms. Fabulous are more likely than not at your local charity performing voluntary tasks.

Volunteering is the ideal way to meet new and interesting people. First of all, you will be around other people who also have "giving" natures and who understand the concept of generosity and compassion. Furthermore, you will see the true nature of a person as he or she interacts with others. As you experience their essence and nature, you will get a glimpse of who they really are as you see their spontaneous responses to others in a variety of circumstances.

There are special moments of compassion, tenderness, and vulnerability during many of your volunteer experiences. These are moments you might just have the opportunity to share with Mr. Wonderful or Ms. Fabulous. From shared moments like these a date opportunity might arise, and from there — who knows? And it all started from the simple act of volunteering.

The spirit of voluntarism and generous individual giving must continue to be the special virtue we exhibit. In that spirit will be found life's finest experiences.

WINFIELD C. DUNN

How can I give my money creatively as a volunteer?

There's more than one way to "skin a cat" and there's more than one way to "give creatively." Cash gifts are most acceptable, but they are not usually the most beneficial to the donor. Gifts of appreciated securities give you, the donor, a full tax deduction for the full market value of the stock on the day of your donation. This type of donation makes it a wiser gift than cash. The charity gets the same amount of money, but you get the benefit of the appreciated value of the stock as an extra tax deduction.

Personal gifts such as charitable remainder trusts and gift annuities can become major estate-planning vehicles for you and your family as well as significant gifts for the charities you love. Life insurance gifts and bequests by wills are truly creative ways to make voluntary contributions.

There are many financial experts in your community to guide you in planned giving. Call your family attorney, CPA, life insurance broker, or development director at your charity for information on charitable giving.

The value in giving is not connected to the amount given — the value is related to the spirit of the giver. And if you can be creative in the way you give, both you and the charities you support will benefit.

The size of the gift to an institution
is not important. No gift is important,
no matter how large, unless it means
something to the one who gives it.

— R. BLAIR SCHREYER

How can I volunteer on weekends?

"What am I going to do this weekend? I sure wish I could do something different and exciting!" Ever find yourself thinking these thoughts on Friday around lunchtime? And what do you do? Like me, probably nothing. What a waste: two more days and another weekend is lost. But thanks to volunteer opportunities, next weekend can be found, and in finding it you just might find yourself.

First, you must decide what area interests you for your weekend volunteer work. Are you interested in volunteering in your local animal shelter? The animal shelters are busiest on Saturdays and always need help with people who are adopting a pet or dropping off an unwanted pet for others to adopt. Would you like to help coach a weekend sports team — baseball, swimming soccer, or tennis? Maybe you would like to work with senior citizens. Retirement centers and nursing homes are an ideal place to volunteer on weekends because they can be lonely times for seniors.

Another lost weekend? Or one that will change your life. The decision is yours. That exciting weekend you've been looking for is just around the corner. Volunteer today and make it a reality.

Volunteering can be an exciting, growing, enjoyable experience. It is truly gratifying to serve a cause, practice one's ideals, work with people, solve problems, see benefits, and know one had a hand in them.

— HARRIET NAYLOR

— 9 —

I've volunteered before but I always drop out. How can I stay excited about volunteering?

Excitement is a by-product of volunteering. Granted, volunteering offers many opportunities for peak moments of excitement. However, like any job (paid or not) there is a necessity for practical daily responsibilities, procedures, rules, and order designed to be followed by the agency or organization for whom you are volunteering. Sometimes this practical side of volunteering discourages us and leads us to drop out.

Initial efforts of volunteering can be times of high intensity, excitement, and expectation. To maintain your commitment to your volunteer job, remember to pace your time and efforts to avoid burnout. A natural tendency in early volunteering is to overextend yourself. Take personal time with your volunteer coordinator and explain exactly what amount of time and energy you have to give in order for you to maintain a level of commitment and excitement about your job. Also, remember that you maintain excitement when you lighten up; keep looking for the humorous side of what you are doing as a volunteer. As long as you can keep laughing, especially at yourself, you won't even think of dropping out.

"I can't do it anymore. It's just too sad for me." These were the words of a long-time volunteer working with AIDS patients. Just as he spoke these words and turned to go out the door of the AIDS clinic, a patient asked him in a loud voice to come back to his bed for a moment. The volunteer walked back to hear these words: "Lighten up, Joe. It's not that bad. Sure, I'm going to die, but you have made my life these last days so much better. In fact, to tell you the truth, before you came, I was already dead. You have given me life, Joe. Without you, I would already be dead. You are my life, Joe. Don't go." And the volunteer stayed.

You don't have to drop out as a volunteer. You only need to change your perception of what is really going on by stopping for a moment and listening to those in need. Their voices will renew your excitement about volunteering. Their lives will inspire you anew.

When people are serving, life is no longer meaningless.

— JOHN W. GARDNER

I'm usually generous to the needy in my community around the holidays. Isn't that enough?

Julie Salmon beautifully tells the true story of Christmas giving in her lovely book The Christmas Tree. A little orphan girl named Anna befriends a tiny fir tree she affectionately refers to by the name "Tree." As she grows into a young girl, she and Tree share the secrets and magic of life together under its wide branches. Anna grows up to become a nun named Sister Anthony and continues to enjoy the peace and solitude she finds in nature with her friend Tree. When Sister Anthony grows into an old woman, she allows her dearest and closest friend to be cut, transported, and decorated with lights and tinsel to become the most celebrated tree in the world, the Christmas tree at Rockefeller Center in New York City. She had learned to love Tree but found a greater love being able to share her love for Tree with others.

This is the greatest lesson to learn from the holiday season of voluntary giving. Giving may begin then, but it does not end there. The love we share with others is only the beginning as we offer "our tree" and share it with others throughout the year.

The spirit of Christmas is always near,
it shines like a beacon throughout the year.
Don't look in a store or high on a shelf,
for sharing and giving are found in yourself.

— Anonymous

— 11 —

How can I stop volunteering?

It's not always easy to say "no" to a cause or an issue you feel strongly about supporting. However, be realistic. Sometimes you should say no. We all have limits regarding what we feel we can successfully contribute as a volunteer. People volunteer for a variety of reasons: a desire to make the world better; a need for new social contacts; a search for self-fulfillment by giving to a cause; or an enhanced work experience. As our life's priorities shift and circumstances change, we may no longer have the desire to continue volunteering. However, instead of dropping out with no explanation, call your volunteer coordinator and explain your circumstances.

Volunteer drop-out can often be linked to an initial burst of over-enthusiasm. A volunteer may offer his or her time and talents for "whatever is needed" only to find that the assigned task does not match their interests or available amount of volunteer time. If this is happening to you, then request a task more suited to your talents or adjust your available amount of volunteer time to fit your schedule.

Saying no is not always the easy way, but it might turn out to be the best way. Many times the important "yes" in our life started with a firm but thoughtful "no." When you are ready to commit as a volunteer, do it. But until then, your best answer is probably, "I just cannot volunteer at this time."

***The usual trouble with volunteers is not
killing them with overwork,
but simply boring them to death.***

— HAROLD J. SEYMOUR

— 12 —

How can I raise money as a volunteer?

For more than thirty years I have been both a professional and volunteer fund-raiser. I love it. Why? Because I do not raise money. All I do is "offer opportunities" for others to give. Since I know a little secret — that the greatest joy in the world is giving — I am fearless as an "opportunity offerer." I give other people the chance to get what they want: joy. I give them that chance by offering them the opportunity to make the world a little better through giving.

To be a good volunteer fund-raiser, you must first have experienced the joy of giving yourself. Once you have been touched by the magic elixir of what happens to you when you help others, you will want to share this experience. You will want to offer people an opportunity to give.

A husband and wife who had given the funds to build a cancer center which was named after them only said, "Thank you for this chance to help others," as they stood there with their family in Ft. Worth, Texas, on dedication day. People want to give. They only need someone to ask them. Could that possibly be you?

Blessed are the money raisers. . .
for in heaven they shall stand
on the right hand of the martyrs.

— JOHN R. MOTT

Does volunteering affect my health?

Physiological responses from volunteering can be measured and charted by physicians in lowered stress levels, heightened immune systems, and better sleep patterns, but there are also immeasurable psychological responses that affect your health as a direct result of volunteering. Volunteers have been studied and it has been found that often during just a few hours of volunteering a person's general physiological demeanor and psychological well-being are so heightened that this has been nicknamed "The Helper's High."

Voluntarism will create a support group with whom you can work, socialize, and see visible results that will magically give your general health a boost. As you are presented with challenges through giving to others you will develop a rapid response and enhancement of your immune system.

Those who give to others think less often of themselves and are less prone to seeking immediate personal gratification. Becoming a giver guarantees you the ability to be present and living in the moment for life's beauty and wonder. This is what health is all about — living a life that has meaning. Volunteering Is a way to get there. Can you really afford any longer not to be on that direct path to health?

Some patients, though conscious that
their condition is perilous, recover their health
simply through the contentment with the
goodness of their physician.

— HIPPOCRATES

Does volunteering affect my happiness?

Cornell University tracked a group of people over a thirty-year period and reported that those who volunteered were happier and healthier than those who did not. It was clearly determined those who volunteered had a greater sense of self-satisfaction, a purpose in life, and they were happier.

Volunteering also significantly allows a reduction of toxic stress in our lives. This gives us feelings of self-acceptance which then allow us to feel compassion and empathy for others. Volunteering releases natural chemicals in our brain called endorphins that produce a feeling of joy and greater clarity, much like the feeling athletes experience during a good workout.

You don't have to change the world to benefit from the happiness derived from volunteering. You can find small ways to serve in your community which correspond with your interests and available time. Happiness is yours for the taking.

Thomas Jefferson and our Founding Fathers declared that we had the right to pursue happiness as free Americans. Where are you in your pursuit? If it has eluded you so far, perhaps the place to start is by making other people happy.

I slept and dreamed that life was happiness.
I awoke and saw that life was service. I served
and found that in service happiness is found.

— Rabindranath Tagore

Does volunteering affect my length of life?

You will be glad to know there is a fountain of youth and it is yours for the taking. Virtually no bad effects result from volunteering. Giving and sharing yourself through voluntarism provides you with a significant reduction in toxic stress chemicals in the body actually reducing stress levels; volunteering decreases your metabolic rate and increases your abilities for a good night's sleep; volunteering also enhances proper functioning of your immune system; and volunteering can lengthen your life.

Medical schools have studied men who volunteer after age sixty-five and those who do not; on average the senior men who volunteer outlive the non-volunteers. This is a medical fact that too many retired men do not know. What a shame! What a waste!

The greatest benefits for a long and healthy life are the spiritual benefits that result from voluntarism. As you become a giver, you will step out into your community with a greater sense of connection to your fellow citizens; you will have a higher sense of appreciation and acceptance of others with a greater clarity about the meaning and purpose of your own life. What a way to spend the rest of your life!

***The life that will be preserved
is the life that is freely given in service
to God and man.***

— ELLEN G. WHITE

How can I deal with a bad experience I once had as a volunteer?

One of the main qualities of learning to be a good volunteer is to be able to forgive quickly and move on to the job at hand for the highest good of the charity. This is not always easy to do when tempers flare and harsh words are spoken in anger, but the rewards of forgiveness are greater than you can possibly imagine.

It is always up to us to be the one who forgives, because if we don't, we are the ones who will pay the price by holding on tightly to resentments. People who have learned the lessons of happiness and joy know that the ability to be present in the moment and enjoy the gifts and lessons of today lies in the ability to forgive everyone they feel has ever harmed them in the past.

A key to life lived to its fullest is forgiveness. There are really no simple solutions to bad experiences as a volunteer, but the simplest and best solution is to forgive and move on. Close the door on your bad volunteer experience and open the door to a more exciting one awaiting you.

Noble deeds and hot baths
are the best cure for depression.

— Debbie Smith

Is there anything I can do to learn how to volunteer?

Nonprofit agencies throughout America offer a variety of training for new volunteers. One agency may offer you a formal induction as a new volunteer while another agency may ask a veteran volunteer to show you on a one-to-one basis the ropes of your new job.

If your volunteer job requires technical training, the agency will incorporate the specialized training for you to learn the skills required to do your job for them. Most long-term international volunteer assignments require extensive training in the cultural, language, and local issues of your host country before you begin your volunteer assignment. Many domestic volunteer jobs also require thorough training, and this is offered to volunteers free of charge.

It is always a good idea to ask for help when you begin any new volunteer job. Be sure to attend training sessions, ask questions, and participate with the other volunteers until you are quite certain of what's required of you. If the agency where you volunteer does not offer training, help them by donating a copy of Tracy Daniel Connors's *The Volunteer Management Handbook*.

Caring must strengthen into commitment and commitment into action if we are to preserve and nurture one of the greatest forces for rebirth and renewal this nation has...voluntarism.

— MARLENE WILSON

Where can I go for some new ways to volunteer?

If you are a seasoned volunteer and are simply looking for a variety of new ways to serve your community, call your local volunteer center for opportunities or call your mayor's office for information on local civic needs. If you are new to the world of volunteering, then find a mentor in the volunteer community to help guide you through the stages of finding a suitable job.

Perhaps the most intriguing idea of all is for you to dream up a new way of volunteering. John van Hengel wanted to feed the hungry in Phoenix in 1967 and he came up with the idea of creating a food bank. His idea grew into first food bank in the world, St. Mary's. This original volunteer idea was followed by Second Harvest, which van Hengel founded in 1979. Second Harvest has become the largest domestic hunger-relief organization in the country. Who knows how many millions of people have received nourishment from these two new ideas of one volunteer in Phoenix?

Do you have a new volunteer idea? Why not take a chance like John van Hengel and try it out today?

If you're not here to serve somebody,
if there's going to be no integrity
to your journey, no honor to it,
then why are you here?

— HARRY BELAFONTE

— 19 —

How can I make volunteering become a good habit?

Volunteering is a process of learned behavior over a lifetime. If you are very lucky, you had parents who established your good habits of voluntarism when you were a child by involving you in community projects but it's never too late to become a volunteer.

Your schedule may require some juggling to make volunteering a priority. Generally, in order to develop a new habit we are required to give up something first. It is when you replace a behavior or activity with another that a habit has the possibility of being formed.

Replacing your current lifestyle with community involvement is not always easy. There are times you may be sitting in your reclining chair on a cold night thinking to yourself, "I think I'll stay home again tonight and watch television." But in your heart, you know staying home watching television again is also a habit. You will learn to get up, put on your coat, and go out as a volunteer to be with people who may not have a home, or a television to watch, and you will see the joy on their faces when you walk in the door. Now that is a good habit! And one you can learn now.

I prefer death to lassitude.
I never tire of serving others.

— Leonardo da Vinci

— 20 —

Can volunteering be an answer to my anger?

According to the American Psychological Association, anger should not be swept under the carpet by simply focusing on something positive. The danger in suppressing anger and turning it inward is that it may cause hypertension, high blood pressure, or depression. However, mental health experts suggest that finding volunteer opportunities in our communities may give us a sense of value and self-worth by shifting our routine and focus from our anger to seeing good and beauty in the world around us.

The next time you need a healthy outlet for your anger, call your volunteer center and see if you can find a weekend job volunteering by helping to plant flowers in a local park or helping to clean trash along a highway. Volunteering is an ideal way to feel a sense of purpose while working through myriad human emotions.

Remember the last time you were really angry? Can you recall the energy and time you wasted? Do you still have a bit of the hurt inside? Why not try something different the next time the anger bug bites? As the blood rushes to your head and your voice raises several decibels in its pitch, why not just stop where you are, leave the scene of the anger, and go solve someone else's problem? This may just be what you need to do.

People who fight fire with fire, usually end up with ashes.

— Abigail Van Buren

— 21 —

Can volunteering help me out of depression?

Combined with good medical treatment, volunteering can help you get out of a state of depression.

Depression is a medical disorder that affects your thoughts, physical health, and behavior, and causes psychic, social, and physical pain. This common and treatable illness affects one in twenty Americans or eleven million people every year. The good news is that when depression is diagnosed and treated properly, a person may return to a happy and vigorous lifestyle within a matter of weeks! 80% of all treatment for depression is successful.

When you have been in treatment for your depression for a few weeks, you may feel like stepping outside your former habits and routines and into your community to volunteer. The time you spend helping others will give you enhanced feelings of self-esteem, and this, coupled with good medical treatment, will put you on the road to health and happiness.

Upon this new foundation of positive self-worth you will build a life anew, centered around helping others. Someone once offered ten rules for getting rid of the blues: "Go out and do something nice for someone else and then repeat it nine times."

Love cures people —
both the ones who give it and
the ones who receive it.

— DR. KARL MENNINGER

I'm a retired middle-class American. What can I do to give back?

Retired senior citizens (like you) are healthier than ever before in history! As a result, your retirement years can be the most productive and fulfilling years of your life. Only ten percent of Americans age sixty-five and older have debilitating health problems to keep them from being active in their communities. If you are part of the healthy ninety percent then your life has just begun — a new life of giving back will be your best years ever!

Now is the time for you as a middle-class American to give back to your community and your country by using the work skills you have developed over a lifetime. Many high schools and groups like Junior Achievement and I Have a Dream solicit professionals from the community to assist in mentoring programs. Nonprofit agencies need your professional contacts to serve their clients needs. Retirement does not mean you are "out of the loop" but rather you are a needed commodity, rich with experiences to offer your community.

There is also an extra benefit of volunteering which awaits you. Medical science now knows that people your age who give back live longer than people who don't! This is especially true for men. Why are you not already volunteering? The benefits are not only to your community but also to you.

***When you stop giving and offering
something to the rest of the world,
it's time to turn out the lights.***

— GEORGE BURNS

Is there any compensation for volunteering my time?

There are ways that you can be compensated for your volunteer efforts. One way is to deduct your car mileage for volunteer activities when filing your federal income taxes. You may also find some select programs for senior citizen volunteers which offer a meal or a minimal financial stipend of $2.00 per hour, or other non-cash incentives.

The Peace Corps volunteer program offers opportunities for graduate school scholarships and fellowships. You will receive a $5,400 readjustment allowance after twenty-seven months of service. The Americorps volunteer program pays a modest living allowance, health insurance, and $4,725 per year.

Corporate America is beginning to offer paid time-off for certain volunteer jobs. Tootsietoy Company in Chicago offers vacation days for volunteer efforts. Charlotte's Nations-Bank offers 8,000 employees two hours each week of paid leave to volunteer at their children's schools.

The true compensation you will receive through your volunteer service is your sense of connection to the world around you, which brings a sense of purpose and joy to your life. No amount of money can buy the benefits generated by becoming a volunteer.

I feel that the greatest reward for doing is the opportunity to do more.

— JONAS SALK

Can volunteering help me build new skills?

Volunteering offers an ideal way to gain experience. General Mills Corporation offered a volunteer program in which 56 percent of its employees said they learned new leadership skills and 36 percent said they had improved their work skills as a direct result of volunteering.

There are a variety of skills to be learned through volunteering which enable you to gain valuable career-related experience. Many employers require hands-on experience with certain skills, and volunteering offers you the chance to learn new skills.

Remember to treat your volunteer job as you would any paid position. Follow the rules, act in a professional and cheerful manner, dress appropriately, and adhere to the guidelines of the agency or organization with whom you are volunteering. Those who stand out as volunteers are often chosen for leadership positions. When you take a leadership role as a volunteer, you assume the responsibility of a project or task and you develop problem solving skills, people skills and the ability to be spontaneous and creative. All these qualities help you develop a high level of self-confidence, making you happier and more successful.

The making of money, the accumulation of material power, is not all there is to living... and the man who misses this truth misses the greatest joy and satisfaction that come into his life — service to others.

— Edward Bok

Can volunteering give me
the child I never had?

There are programs readily available for building relationships with children not your own. One of the largest mentoring organizations is Big Brothers and Big Sisters of America. Others include Boys and Girls Clubs of America and the Boy Scouts and Girl Scouts. Most of the participating youth in these programs are between the ages of ten and eighteen years old. A lengthy study of the Big Brothers and Big Sisters program provided amazing results. Researchers found after extensive study that 46 percent of the children in the program were less likely to use illegal drugs, 27 percent less likely to begin using alcohol, 52 percent less likely to skip school, and 37 percent less likely to skip a class.

You may choose to volunteer your time in foster grandparent programs and help younger children, or mentor at-risk youth. Many prenatal hospital nurseries offer volunteer opportunities for loving people to rock newborns at various times throughout the day. You may enjoy being a Scout leader, a Sunday-school teacher, or a neighborhood babysitter for after-school care. Summer camps need counselors, fraternity and sorority houses need house parents, juvenile detention centers need wise and loving role models. In serving, you may just finally meet the child you never had. A child who needs your love, and a child who will give you back the love you need so much.

The greatest gift I ever had from God.
I call him Dad.

— Anonymous

Can volunteering be a way for me to have an avocation?

You can find an outlet for every talent and interest in your life through volunteering. Are you a weekend chef or gardener? Would you like to use those skills and talents in your community? Offer your skills to an organization that needs those skills.

If you're searching for an avocation, then volunteering can introduce you to a variety of opportunities to share your energy and interest within miles and minutes of your own home. Decide what interests you and determine the amount of time you'd like to volunteer each month, and then go searching! If you enjoy storytelling, then call a senior citizens' home to volunteer your time to entertain an appreciative and captive audience. Maybe you would enjoy coaching softball with a group of at-risk youth on weekends. Perhaps you would be better suited to building stage sets for your local community theater group. There is an endless list of available opportunities for you to enjoy yourself, feel needed, and get to your community through volunteering. Your acts of generosity and kindness will make the world a kinder, gentler place because of your participation. And you just might gain a new avocation and outlook on life.

The way not to live a monotonous life is to live for others.

— FULTON J. SHEEN

— 27 —

Can volunteering be a way for me to use my creativity?

Volunteering provides endless opportunities for sharing your gifts and talents with the world.

Your creative talents are a gift to any charity. You can virtually choose a cause or community need to support. Would you like to teach dance to at-risk youth? Are you interested in reading your poetry to senior citizens? Do you have the talents to organize an art auction fund-raiser for a ballet troupe to travel to another city? Can you spare an evening to sing for some terminally ill children at your local hospital? Are you a carpenter who can help Habitat for Humanity build a house?

Creative talents that do not find expression are diminished. Unused, they will dissipate. If you do not have an outlet for your creativity, volunteering will offer you receptive audiences to appreciate your efforts. What a way to have it all! An audience for your creativity and a way to bring joy to others through the use of your natural talents.

A bell is not a bell until you ring it.
A song is not a song until you sing it.
Love in your heart is not put there to stay.
Love is not love until you give it away.

— Oscar Hammerstein

Can volunteering help me feel needed?

Being needed is a basic human desire. We need to feel connected to the world outside ourselves. I often wonder who needs who more? Is it the volunteer? Or the one receiving the benefits from the volunteer's efforts? We all need each other. Often our materialistic and chaotic lifestyles don't offer us many opportunities for true intimacy and connection. But volunteering with people who need us gives us all this, and more.

Even as you are reading this book, people need you. There are shut-ins right now who are hungry for a small meal and a few minutes of conversation. Our hospitals are full of people who are feeling pain and loneliness as they lie in cold hospital surroundings. Juvenile delinquency centers are filled with teenagers who are in desperate need of someone who will listen. You can volunteer one evening a week and make a profound difference in someone's life — and your own.

All of us "need" to be "needed". Volunteering is your quickest way to fulfill this '"need."

It is one of the most beautiful
compensations of this life
that no man can sincerely
try to help another
without helping himself.

— RALPH WALDO EMERSON

I'm bedridden. Can I volunteer?

Absolutely! All you need to become a volunteer is a giving heart and willingness. There is always a high need in volunteer organizations for thank-you notes to be promptly written and mailed to those who have contributed to their cause. Call a local charity in your neighborhood to volunteer your time to hand-write their thank-you notes. You might also volunteer to make reminder telephone calls for an agency's volunteer staff for special events.

Opening your heart to others actually opens your own life to love. You may find that new friends will come to your bedside to share news about their personal lives. The truth is, we all need each other. The busier life becomes, the more isolated people feel. Your being bedridden may be the ideal opportunity for someone you contacted as a volunteer to come sit with you for your mutual companionship.

Lying in bed day after day requires creativity on your part to find ways to think less often of your physical disability and pain. A volunteering job creates ways for you to focus outside yourself instead of dwelling on your limitations. And in a true Zen way, this brings you what you need: relief from your boredom and a substitute for your pain.

The greater part of our happiness
or misery depends on our disposition
and not our circumstances.

— Martha Washington

Can I successfully volunteer my time with a member of the opposite sex?

You will learn a great deal about the opposite sex through voluntarism. I suggest that you volunteer with a charity with an equally balanced number of men and women volunteers, and you will see the joy and spirit of cooperation in the group. In fact, you may be surprised at the laughter and lack of self-consciousness created when a group of men and women gather for a common purpose and goal — it's as if the group becomes one large family during the time they are together. Gender is not an issue in volunteering.

As far as working with a member of the opposite sex who has a need in the community, I believe men and women each bring their best qualities to situations on an equal basis. A hungry child doesn't care if the person who provides the meal is female. A homeless person doesn't care about the gender of the person who donated the money that provided him or her a place to eat, sleep, and shower for the night.

Love is greater than gender, race, color, creed, age, and sex. We are at our highest and best when we are giving, and even transcend our own weaknesses as humans when our time, talent, and treasures are given regardless of whether we are male or female.

**The vocation of every man and woman
is to serve other people.**

— Leo Tolstoy

Can I heal my own pain by volunteering my time with others?

Support of others is an ideal way to heal your pain. Find a level of volunteering, however, that does not require you to give more than you have to offer.

There is a certain therapeutic value in getting "outside" ourselves by placing other's needs above our own for a period of time. You will find that your pain diminishes during those few hours of volunteering as you give of yourself to others. As time passes you will find the value of your own pain, which makes you more compassionate toward others. Time heals all human pains, but by giving a little of yourself away in acts of kindness, you will find the time frame is speeded up and your healing more complete.

Pain is something we all must bear at some time in our lives as humans. How we bear it, however, is totally up to us. We can let it become a burden that sinks our ship of life, or we can allow our pain to be healed as we become volunteers helping others.

Help thy brother's boat across and, lo!
thine own has reached the shore.

— HINDU PROVERB

Can I learn patience from volunteering?

I often wonder if the word "patience" is not a combination of the words "pay" and "attention." Perhaps the magic and mystery of voluntarism is learning to put aside your personal needs and wants just long enough to pay attention to the needs and wants of another human being.

The ability to focus outside yourself requires a degree of patience with yourself and others. It is a developed skill you can learn with practice.

It is easy to a see lack of patience in other people especially in rush-hour traffic as they shake their fists in the air screaming inaudible words at passing cars. It's not always easy to see a lack of patience in yourself. Volunteering is an ideal school for teaching you the virtue of patience. I recommend you begin your "patience lessons" by working with a highly skilled volunteer capable of teaching you by his or her own example. Watch them as they quietly hold the hand of a disabled child with tenderness. Stand closely as they read to a senior citizen in a nursing home. Watching others exhibit patience and gentle rapport will infuse you with a gift that will sustain you all the days of your life — by giving the gift of patience.

We're put on this earth
not to see through each other
but to see each other through.

— ANONYMOUS

— 33 —

Is volunteering my money really enough?

Yes, if you give from your heart, not your head.

There are endless choices of ways you can spend your money. You can take exotic holidays, buy expensive goods and services, or you can give to good causes with the intention of making the world better. Giving money to charitable organizations is a benevolent act that certainly benefits others. It also gives you a sense of satisfaction knowing that you have done a good deed. Does this mean that volunteering your money is enough? Probably not, unless the money is given with no strings attached and given freely from your heart.

The wonderful thing about money is that it's a symbol of what you are committed to and what you love. When a child asks you for an allowance raise, the request is not for more money, but really for a statement from you that you are still committed in love to the child. A gift of money is the same thing. It is your way of saying, "I am committed in love to what this charity is trying to do in the world."

What are you committed to? Maybe the answer is really in your checkbook.

"What I gave, I have.
What I spent, I had.
What I left, I lost by not giving it."

— EPITAPH OF CHRISTOPHER CHAPMAN

— 34 —

Do "real men" volunteer?

America was founded with the strength of a man's back and his common sense, along with the raw courage and dignity of the woman who stood beside him. Behind the desire of a man to step out of his role as husband and father to help his community is an understanding of his connection with the world around him and how his participation can make a difference.

The world still needs the strength of a man's back and his common sense. It is also in desperate need of the raw courage and dignity women bring as volunteers. Those who volunteer, whether male or female, know the meaning of the word "humanity" because they have stood toe-to-toe with suffering and sorrow.

Where is it that we make real men? Ironically, it is not just on the battlefields of sports and war and Wall Street. Real men are made out of the stuff of tears and struggle and pain.

You want to be a real man? There is something better than Charles Atlas to help you become all you can be. It is called volunteering.

Man can see his reflection on water
only when he bends down close to it;
and the heart of man, too,
must lean down to the heart of his fellow;
then it will see itself within his heart.

— HASIDIC PROVERB

I am a woman who works from 9 to 5. Can I still volunteer as my mother did?

Today women are being heard, but it is within the confines of a world that includes both family and a job. This new world is one that appears to have no time for volunteering as mother did.

Despite how busy life has become, volunteering is a beneficial way for women to express themselves in their communities. More and more women are working 9 to 5 jobs as divorce rates and the cost of living continue to soar. It is important to note, however, that women today are like the pioneer women who united to end their isolation and inequality in the world around them; the busier women are today, the more isolated they become. And this is an isolation that volunteering can overcome.

There are modern solutions for successful volunteering to fit the schedules of contemporary women. Learn to invent new ways and times to fit volunteering into your busy life. Consider volunteering on weekends. Use your education, work experience, problem-solving, nurturing, and intuitive skills as valuable volunteer assets to be given via the telephone and correspondence. Your mother would be proud of how you use volunteering to help make today's world a better place in which to live, and your mother would be proud of your innovative ways of volunteering.

Twas her thinking of others
made you think of her.

— ELIZABETH BARRETT BROWNING

Can I successfully volunteer with a person who is not my age?

There is wisdom and grace in a grandmother's tenderness, just as surely as there is exuberant joy in the face of an infant. Volunteering offers you the rich opportunity to work with all ages.

It's easy to say to yourself that you feel you have nothing to offer to someone older or younger than yourself. I am asking you to open your heart and close your eyes to the factor of age, and you will see that you are on a spiritual journey that makes the whole world your family. Age, therefore, is not a factor.

Do you think Mother Teresa saw age as a factor when she did her ministry? No, she saw a human being in need regardless of his or her age and worked with that person to help relieve their suffering. Mother Teresa was a mature adult but most of her patients were much younger — and this did not stop her.

Need is ageless. You can be successful as a volunteer with a person of any age if your prime motive for volunteering is service to others.

We seldom stop to think how many people's lives are entwined with our own. It is a form of selfishness to imagine that every individual can operate on his own or can pull out of the general stream and not be missed.

— IVY BAKER PRIEST

How can I volunteer and exercise at the same time?

Your local newspaper generally advertises upcoming community events that offer you an opportunity to volunteer and exercise at the same time. Walkathons are extremely popular in towns all across America. These exercise-related fund-raisers came to public attention in the early 1980s when AIDS activists were raising money at a citywide, grassroots level. To participate in these popular events, you will be asked to secure a pledge/donation from friends and businesses for each mile you complete.

Because of the walkathons' extreme success, charities have extended the walkathon theme to include jogathons for runners, hikeathons for nature lovers, bowlathons for bowlers, driveathons for golfers, danceathons for dancers, swimathons for swimmers, jumpathons for trampoline enthusiasts, and rideathons for horse lovers. These popular fund raising projects draw in exercise enthusiasts from their communities gaining new support and new financial resources that they would not otherwise have received.

Would you like to lose weight, look better, feel better, sleep better, and basically become a new physical you? Maybe the answer is not just better eating habits or joining a health club — it just might be volunteering!

The act of volunteering is
an assertion of individual worth.

— Edward C. Linderman

SECTION II

Volunteering and Life

Volunteering: A noble thought turned into action.

— MANUEL ARANGO

Will my volunteering make any real difference?

Yes, volunteering will make a difference in your life and in the many lives you will touch because of your giving. Like a pebble thrown into a pond whose ripples flutter to the shore, every act of kindness you display creates a chain of positive good into the lives of thousands of people you will never meet, and continues into future generations!

Our cultural tendency for immediate gratification often blinds us to our own effectiveness. You can volunteer in ways that will make small changes over time, affecting the long-term greater good of your community and world. Taking a longer look at your voluntarism can help you understand your small role in the great scheme of making this a better world for everyone.

Did Mother Teresa's life as a volunteer among the oppressed make a difference? Did Princess Diana's life as a volunteer really touch the lives of other people around the world? You and I both know these two women made a difference. You can too. What are you waiting for?

I have been the recipient of love and service,
therefore I can love and serve.
There is great satisfaction in service
to others, in... seeing people and
their conditions change.

— CLARENCE E. HODGES

Can volunteering be a spontaneous occurrence?

While driving south of Paris on a hot August day, I stopped at a rest area in my rental car. When I went to start it again, it would not respond. Not knowing what to do, I asked a couple parked in their travel trailer to help me. Although they only spoke Dutch, they came over to help, but without success. A German-speaking couple then came over and the four of them proceeded to attempt to decipher the French car manual. Forty-five minutes later we also attracted a Belgian truck driver, and several others. No one could speak English, but no one left and everybody continued to volunteer their help. Finally, the truck driver discovered the secret, and the car started, to the cheers of our gathering of Good Samaritans.

As this United Nations assembly of spontaneous volunteers adjourned and my wife and I sped off, I knew finally how we could establish world peace forever. Give us all something for which to volunteer and all the artificial boundaries of hate and fear and distrust will dissolve into that exciting moment when one human being says to another, "Can I help?"

*Life is an exciting business
and most exciting when
it is lived for others.*

— Helen Keller

How can I have fun volunteering?

The ultimate fun we had as children was to just be ourselves. Volunteering can offer you a way back to that carefree time. We need to have this in our lives as adults, and that inner freedom to have fun is what you can experience while volunteering at a circus for special children, or the soup kitchen, or on a jogathon. This is where you can bring a smile to another simply by putting on the clown's mask, serving a bowl of soup, or running in the outdoors for a cause.

Stepping outside yourself and into your community is a way to have fun. Certainly fun is a relative term. For some, volunteering at a zoo on Saturday is fun. For others it may be painting watercolor tattoos on children at a local street fair or seeing the smile on the face of a child (or adult) learning to read. There are endless opportunities to participate in playful projects in your immediate neighborhood. The rewards for community volunteering are endless and you are guaranteed to bring smiles to others while you play with them — just as you did as a child — and just have fun.

I don't know what your destiny will be,
but one thing I know:
the only ones among you who will be really
happy are those who have sought
and found how to serve.

— Albert Schweitzer

How does volunteering relate to my real purpose in life?

Wisdom is born from life's rich experiences. Scholars, poets, and theologians agree that losing oneself through benevolence toward others is a way to find our life's true purpose. There is a renaissance of simplification in living as people search for meaning in their personal lives.

Community involvement through voluntarism offers people like you an opportunity to participate in efforts toward self-fulfillment, self-esteem, and greater joy in your life. The United States is the wealthiest country in the world although we only have 5 percent of the world's population. Our culture hungers for more meaning and purpose in life and volunteering is a way to shift our focus from money to purpose and satisfaction.

The United States spent an estimated $500 billion for gifts during the 1997 Christmas season. This amazing amount of money could restructure our entire society! Voluntarism is an alternative for people looking for more meaning in their lives, especially during the busy holiday season. Many people are planning to spend future holidays by donating their time and money to soup kitchens, delivering gift baskets to shut-ins, organizing food drives, and baking pies for the disabled. There is a hunger for meaning in life. Volunteering your time, treasures, and talent is one of the best ways for you to find that meaning you seek.

*We make a living by what we do,
but we make a life by what we give.*

— Winston Churchill

Does volunteering relate to how the universe works?

The highest universal law apart from gravity is the law of cause and effect. This immutable law is woven throughout every religion and culture throughout time. The Judeo-Christian faith embraces cause and effect by teaching, "A man reaps what he sows." Giving and receiving, like cause and effect, are part of the endless circle of life. It is you who must put the laws of cause and effect and giving and receiving into your own life, since you are the beneficiary of the universal laws.

My question to you is, "How good can you stand it?" Volunteering offers you an unlimited abundance of joy, health, longevity, love, and self-esteem. In order for you to receive these precious gifts, you must first offer yourself as a volunteer to serve others. Yes, you will reap what you sow in thought, words and deed. A heart that is open and eager to love is a heart that will know what it feels like to be loved and to soar with the eagles.

There is a degree of personal sacrifice and self-forgetting involved in giving of yourself as a volunteer. However, the law of cause and effect knows your sacrifice and delivers back to you a higher order of personal reward. Giving requires a degree of humility that leads us to a road of inner peace and true joy.

***God has given us two hands –
one to receive with
and the other to give with.***

— Billy Graham

What can volunteering do for my soul?

If we listen carefully, our souls will tell us what they need. Volunteering is a true adventure for our souls because it provides ways for us to serve others and find purpose in today's busy and materialistic society. Helping others actually infuses our souls with a personal moral cleansing and gives us clarity of understanding of the world around us. Truly, volunteering is a soulful experience of the highest form.

A degree of spirituality is involved in volunteering as we strive to be of service to a cause or community need. This spirituality requires a certain ordinariness that reveals our true character and the vulnerability of being fully human. Our soul is attentive to this spiritual quality. Volunteering is a form of communion with the universe as we step out of self in faith to help others and in so doing, feed our own souls.

As we search for life's often complex answers, volunteering is a way for us to free ourselves from our anxiety and refocus on our souls. And, as if by magic, the answers to life's questions come to us, in unexpected moments, as we help others.

Some tension is necessary for the soul to grow,
and we can put that tension to good use.
We can look for every opportunity
to give and receive love, to appreciate nature,
to heal our wounds and the wounds of others,
to forgive, and to serve.

— JOAN BORYSEMKO

How can volunteering help me face death?

Volunteering helps you face life and it will help you face the issue of your own mortality. Being fully engaged offers you a life rich with truth instead of a life filled with fantasy and escape. You can derive so many extraordinary benefits from volunteering your time, talent and treasures with others that you will experience a life free from self-obsession and worry about your mortality.

We all want to leave something behind, a token of our attempt to make the world a little better. You may be able to leave your legacy by donating enough money to have a hospital wing or public building named after you. Or you may leave your mark on this earth because you gave your time to deliver meals to shut-ins, offered service in your place of worship, or worked in the civic affairs of your community.

Live today as if were the last day of your life. Wouldn't it be wonderful if your last glorious days were spent loving others by volunteering yourself. As Steven Levine put it so well, "If you were going to die soon and had only one phone call you could make, who would you call and what would you say? And why are you waiting?"

Build your life brick upon brick.
Live a life of truth,
And you will look back on a life of truth.
Live a life of fantasy,
And you will look back on delusion.

— ANONYMOUS

Can volunteering bring excitement to my life?

What does excitement mean to you? If it means unprecedented joy at having your life filled with reward and satisfaction, then the answer is "yes." If it means sustained levels of energy and a long, healthy lifespan, then volunteering is the very definition of genuine and long-lasting excitement.

Our culture is filled with schemes and scams to entertain you with glitzy glamour, but you may find that these fleeting activities make your own life seem shallow and empty. Volunteering your time, talent and treasures in your community is a higher form of connection to a level of excitement that speaks to your soul. Your life is certainly what you make it, and it is up to you to step out of your comfort zone and create moments that allow your spirit to soar.

I challenge you to find ways to express your excitement, instead of looking for ways to find excitement. Become a volunteer as a participant instead of being a couch-potato observer. Your volunteering will lead you places that will change your life and make this world a better place. Welcome to the most exciting journey of your life — volunteering.

The most enthusiastic givers in life
are the real lovers of life. They experience
the soul-joy that comes from responding
with the heart rather than the head.

— HELEN STEINER RICE

Can volunteering give me an opportunity to experience sacred moments?

Volunteering is a perfect opportunity for you to step outside your role as a wife or husband, employee or employer, parent or child, and to reach a new and poignant understanding of your own capabilities for compassion and vulnerability. By giving of yourself you find new strengths and courage to go beyond what you thought you were capable of doing. By stretching the wings of your soul you will take flight and know the beauty and tenderness of that sacred moment when you help another human being.

Volunteering offers you the opportunity to be a part of the magic of life as you experience sacred moments. When you volunteer you will have a perspective about what is important in life and what is not. Step out of yourself long enough to see the day-to-day issues many people face and you will become optimistic and grateful for your own lifes circumstances. It is then that life will have a sweeter and deeper meaning to you.

Volunteering opens you up to many new human experiences, but most of all it exposes you to sacred moments that bring true meaning to your life.

The words take on their true meaning
when we see them as verbs
more than nouns:
volunteer, love, God.

— SUE VINEYARD

Can volunteering fill my life with meaning?

In your search for life's meaning, volunteering offers concrete actions. Volunteering will greatly enhance your sense of personal satisfaction and give you a greater ability to cope with crises, as well as a greater empathy for others.

Gratitude is a by-product of selfless giving. This country is the wealthiest nation on earth, renowned for our efficient problem-solving skills. Americans have inherent good fortune that can only be increased by devoting ourselves to others. We can find meaning in life by being grateful for our many gifts and resources; our lives will be enriched by choosing gratitude over greed.

Victor Frankl taught us how to find meaning in our lives in his book Man's *Search for Meaning*, written in a Nazi concentration camp where he found that everything can be taken from us except our spirit, wherein we find meaning in our lives. He observed others keeping their spirit to the end as they gave away their last piece of bread.

Create meaning in your life instead of waiting for it to find you. Take an active community role now! Lose yourself as a volunteer in a project and let it amaze you with its meaningful rewards.

A life devoid of service to others
is a life devoid of meaning.

— Marianne Williamson

Does God want us to volunteer?

The question I ask you is, "What demonstration of your faith can you offer God?" I believe God wants you to live your life as if all the choices you make will make an "eternal" difference in the world around you. You have been given free will to guide and direct your own destiny. God's love is ever present and you are being given direction — even now. Take time away from your habits and routines long enough to stop and listen to the whispering of the small still voice within. Every day you are presented with choices to offer yourself in ways that influence your life and the world in which you live.

Throughout recorded history saints, prophets, and apostles have demonstrated great faith and humility by heeding God's calling. You are given that same choice. Faith can be understood as a "Fantastic Adventure In Trusting Him."

Yes, I believe God wants you to volunteer. I also believe He will give you the strength and courage to do so. The lessons you will learn by becoming a giver will be based upon the divine principle of love, which is the language of the heart. Remember, you can't out-give God. All the love you give to others will come back to you in ways and in an abundance you have never imagined.

In nothing do men more
nearly approach the Gods,
than by doing good
for their fellow man.

— Cicero

SECTION III

Volunteering and Others

Others!

— WILLIAM BOOTH

How can I volunteer with children?

Neglected babies often refuse to eat and often die when treatment is forced upon them. But neglected babies held, rocked, and loved — even by a stranger — will respond to nourishment and begin to bounce back. Give a neglected baby the arms of a loving volunteer who rocks him or her and I will show you a baby on the road back to life.

Children desperately need your love, time, and guidance. There are currently fifteen million children and young people in the United States without an ongoing relationship with a caring adult or mentor, a safe place to learn and grow, or basic skills for a healthy life.

How can you help change these negative statistics? You can volunteer by helping to provide babies and infants with the medications and vaccinations they require, helping build play areas and offering organized after-school activities. Perhaps you can persuade companies to give their employees time off for volunteer work with children in the community. Call your local volunteer center, child welfare agency, school board, or city council member for advice about ways you can volunteer with our nation's most precious asset — our children. Just one child's life is too much to waste.

The soul is healed by being with children.

— FEODOR DOSTOEVSKI

How can I volunteer with older adults?

Today the population of America is increasingly weighted in the direction of older adults; but in spite of this fact these Americans are often neglected or forgotten. Never before in history have our elders needed us more. Yet never before have we turned our heads away more often.

Volunteering with seniors is a rewarding job, but Western society does not revere its elderly the way Eastern cultures have throughout history. Overlooking our elderly has been Western society's loss. You can benefit from the wit and wisdom from the senior citizens in your community — they have more to offer you than you can ever give to them. Serving senior citizens can be a rewarding experience that will change your life. It is hard to believe how we have neglected this valuable opportunity.

Communities organize events for senior citizens. Your local newspaper often has listings of organizations you can contact. Many cities organize ongoing animal therapy in which pets are taken to retirement homes, hospitals, and other facilities where residents benefit from interaction with the animals. Many churches organize transportation for seniors to and from their worship services. Schools and learning centers teach classes for seniors without the pressure of testing or grades.

Meals on Wheels is active as a national program for the preparation and delivery of meals to those seniors who are house-bound after a hospital stay or have needs on a more regular basis. This volunteer job is more than the delivery of a hot meal to someone. It is a warm smile, a familiar face, and a kind word to someone older who is in need.

You can volunteer with older adults today. Why are you waiting? A life-enriching experience for you is only a few volunteer hours away.

The volunteer has become a major force in our lives... because it is not possible for a man to live separated from others. We are involved in each other's lives, not by choice but by necessity.

— NILS SCHWEIZER

How can I volunteer with disabled people?

There is a need to serve those with disabilities. Currently there are 7.1 million chronically disabled Americans: by definition the term "chronically disabled" refers to people who require long-term care or people who cannot take care of themselves for at least three months.

You don't need to look very far to find a place to volunteer with the disabled. Your local hospital can give you information about rehabilitation hospitals that accept volunteer services. If you have an area in which you feel you would like to volunteer, call them. For example, you might volunteer to read for the blind, work with cerebral palsy children or adults, cook for a person living with cancer, or volunteer to do art therapy with the chronically mentally ill. You will never find a shortage of volunteer opportunities within miles of your own home.

"There but for the grace of God go I." If that thought has never crossed your mind, then it is time it did. These clichés are valid: "You are your brother's keeper," and "The bell tolls for thee."

Giving frees us from the familiar
territory of our own needs
by opening our minds
to the unexplored worlds occupied
by the needs of others.

— BARBARA HAND HERRERA

How can I work with uneducated people?

You are educated but many of your neighbors, young and old, are not. They need help. You might be the person who can help them out of the closeted nightmare of illiteracy.

Volunteering to help adults learn to read is a rewarding pursuit that can give you much personal satisfaction. There is tremendous need worldwide for literacy programs. The U.S. Department of Education reports that forty million Americans (20 percent of the population) have only rudimentary reading and writing skills. This group of citizens can locate specific facts in a newspaper article but cannot write a letter to complain about an error in their monthly utility bill. Many so-called "menial" or "entry level" positions require a fundamental understanding of reading and writing: these positions are the foundations of our complex business world. Illiteracy weakens these foundations and thus affects the financial underpinnings of us all.

Literacy standards have changed in the last sixty years. If you graduated from the sixth grade during the Depression, you were considered literate. Today if you graduate from high school you are considered barely literate! Adults who have stepped across the threshold of personal shame and broken the silence of illiteracy have become zealots for education and literacy. Those who overcome illiteracy are instilled with hope and self-esteem, and you will see the joy in the faces of those you help make this step forward. It is a joy that is breathtaking, a powerful elixir of self-esteem.

There are national literacy programs organized at the local level. If you are interested in finding a local community literacy program to volunteer your time, call 800-USA-LEARN or call your local volunteer center or mayor's office for information.

Illiteracy is holding America back. We cannot afford it as a nation and you cannot afford it as a citizen.

Volunteering creates a national character in which the community and the nation take on a spirit of compassion, comradeship, and confidence.

— Brian O'Connell

Does the family that volunteers together, stay together?

Here is one way to stem the flood of divorces which are threatening "the traditional family unit". A strong family unit has been part our foundation as a nation and may be the key to our future. Can volunteering as a family be a possible direction for more family unity, or at the very least, an activity for family harmony?

American families seem to be on a trend toward making volunteering a family matter of prime concern. This may be one of the brightest lights yet in the harsh light of divorce. Let's hope this light gets ever brighter in the years ahead.

According to a 1993 Gallup poll, one-third of all American households reported that volunteering as a family unit was part of their family life together. Their activities included working with seniors, youth groups, and their chosen church affiliation. Almost half the reporting families volunteered in sports or school programs, and a third were directly involved with environmental programs in their local communities. One quarter of the families were serving the homeless in some capacity.

Volunteering together as a family is a powerful experience that possibly can result in family cohesiveness and stability. When your children see you showing kindness and compassion to those in need, it instills a sense of community responsibility in them and they will grow to be adults capable of compassion, sensitivity toward social issues, and individual autonomy. Volunteering also teaches children self-confidence and gives them opportunities to meet people from diverse ethnic origins and age ranges.

Can volunteering together keep families together? It seems to be doing a better job than most other remedies. Why not try it with your family today?

I have tried to live my life as my mother would have wished.
She taught me as a boy that service is the highest duty in the world.
I believed her then, and I believe her now.
I have tried to follow her teaching.

— HENRY FORD

Do friends become better friends by volunteering together?

Volunteering with a friend enhances the quality of your friendship by establishing a purpose beyond socializing and small talk. It will give you language by which you can understand each other through efforts directed at a common goal and by using the highest and best of your God-given talents and the most intimate spiritual gifts you have to share with one another.

Life's hectic pace does not easily provide bonding experiences with friends. At one time, in simpler days, parents were more active with their children's education by attending regular PTA meetings. The children's parents were often friends and socialized and volunteered together on committees and projects to support the children's school. Today parents are often too busy to even meet their children's teachers during the school year, much less be friends with the parents of their children's friends.

It is up to you to find a place to volunteer that will enhance your friendships new and old; you'll see your collaborative contribution with others makes a difference in the world around you. You will find that your friendships will become deeper and richer because you share altruistic goals together. And you will realize only later that these are the true friends you can count on when you need them the most.

Friendship consists in forgetting what one gives and remembering what one receives.

— Alexandre Dumas the Younger

Can a neighborhood change by neighbors volunteering together?

America was built on a pioneering spirit, which meant that when your neighbor's barn burned to the ground, you and the other neighbors quickly had a volunteer "barn raising" that built the barn back.

The very essence and nature of voluntarism is the spirit of cooperation that makes a difference in your neighborhood, city, state, country, and world. Certainly you and your neighbors can help improve your neighborhood through the organization of a neighborhood watch, by scrubbing graffiti from walls, collecting trash along the sides of streets, and keeping an eye out for children in danger.

Natural disasters unite neighborhoods and neighboring cities into massive armies working together to provide shelter during floods, tornados, hurricanes, and droughts. In quieter times neighbors gather their talent and time for daily needs such as child care, help to needy families who have lost a family member or suffer from illness, or errands and meal care for housebound senior citizens. It is the grass-roots voluntarism that serves the common, everyday needs of a neighborhood which is love in its highest and purest form.

As soon as public service ceases to be the chief business of the citizens, and they would rather serve with their money than with their persons, the State is not far from its fall.

— JEAN-JACQUES ROUSSEAU

Professional athletes make so much money! Do they give back to the world?

Professional athletes receive some of the highest salaries in the world, and yes, many of them do give back to the world.

David Robinson, the center for the San Antonio Spurs basketball team, was selected in 1996 as one the fifty greatest players in NBA history. He and his wife, Valerie, have pledged what is believed to be the largest single donation by any professional athlete — a $5 million gift — to help inner-city youth in San Antonio, Texas.

Major-league baseball players united their charitable efforts in 1996 to form the Players Trust for Children and raised $1 million by donating at least two percent of their licensing incomes to help start the ongoing trust.

The list of good voluntary deeds by professional athletes is endless. Sure, they make a lot of money, but many of them give a lot of money and time back. You might not make as much money as they do, but how much of what you have are you giving back? Three cheers for these generous professional athletes. Can we give as many cheers for you?

We want to take kids and mold them into leaders and this is going to be a phenomenal opportunity to do it.

— David Robinson

Can giving teddy bears really make a difference?

Ask that question at Children's Memorial Hospital in Chicago, Illinois. Gladys Holm who died in 1996 at the age of eighty-six was known at Children's Memorial as "The Teddy Bear Lady." She was a retired secretary living alone in a modest apartment in Evanston, Illinois, who took pleasure in bringing sick children teddy bears to brighten their spirits. When she died, she left the hospital $18 million to be used for medical research for diseases of the heart! The teddy bears were her opportunity to visit sick children and find out about their families' money situations — if a family had no money to pay for treatments, Gladys took care of the bills. She always did it anonymously.

Miss Holm did not tell the world about her great wealth. She had been the secretary to the founder of American Hospital Supply, Foster McGraw (himself one of America's great philanthropists). She had been given stock options with American Hospital Supply when the company went public in 1951, and her stocks continued to soar. Her little secret of giving away teddy bears helped save lives, and her generous donation upon her death will impact the lives of thousands of children for years to come.

To insure the continuity of philanthropy,
we must instill in kids the values and attitudes
that will enable them to see charity
as a vital part of their lives.

— Mary Leonard

I'm in my fifties and a billionaire.
What can I do to make a difference?

He was fifty-nine, a billionaire, and as usual, full of surprises. As he stepped to the microphone in New York City, the world knew he had already amassed a fortune from his twenty-four-hour news network (CNN) and other innovative enterprises. He had captained a winning America's Cup team and had been chosen by Time magazine as Man of the Year.

The audience did not know that from December 31, 1996, until that evening, September 18, 1997, his personal net worth had increased from $2.2 billion to $3.2 billion. They also did not know that his surprise announcement was to raise a positive clamor for volunteer philanthropy heard around the world. This billionaire stepped up to the microphone and announced that he was making a $1 billion gift to United Nations programs: $100 million a year for a decade.

This eccentric billionaire had asked himself a question before that dramatic moment in New York City, and it is a question all of us need to ask ourselves whether we are rich or poor: "What is enough?" Ted Turner answered that question with the simple answer that he had enough and wanted voluntarily to share the rest with others around the world. What an inspiration! Thanks again for another surprise, Ted. We will await your next!

There is no greater joy
than giving to worthy causes.

— TED TURNER

I'm seventy and living on Social Security. What can I do?

People are retiring earlier and living longer than ever before in the history of civilization. America's over-fifty-five population is expected to double from thirty-four million to sixty-four million by 2030, which will be twice the size of the younger population. Statistics project that only 5 percent of seniors can expect to require home care, nursing, and fewer than 20 percent will be unable to actively volunteer in their communities.

Volunteering offers seniors on Social Security the deep personal satisfaction of using their business skills and life experiences. Certain large metropolitan cities such as Los Angeles and Atlanta offer a variety of paid volunteer opportunities to lower-income seniors with stipends of $2 per hour or $3,000 to $5,000 per year. Certain programs even provide the cost of transportation and a meal for its senior volunteers.

Altruistic work leads to improved health and emotional well-being for older adults. Volunteering is tailor-made for seniors who seek greater longevity, enhanced functioning for their immune systems, improved cardiovascular circulation, healthier sleep, as well as a greater connection to their fellow human beings and to God. What a bargain. You get back more than you give and end up with a richer, fuller, healthier, and longer life.

There never was a person
who did anything worth doing
that did not receive more than he gave.

— Henry Ward Beecher

I'm a teenager with a weekly allowance. What can I do?

You are a member of the largest generation that has ever lived at one time. One billion young people between the ages of fifteen and twenty-four are living on earth today. It is you and your generation who are the hope of the world. Your values will shape the destiny of all future generations.

"What can I do?" and my answer is "Become a giver! Teach your friends to become givers! Scream it from the rooftops!" As the world population continues to grow and vital earth resources and government support begin to lessen, the need for voluntarism will increase on local, national, and international levels.

Since you are a teenager with a weekly allowance, I recommend you put some of your weekly money into a jar (even if it's only a quarter) and allocate it to be pledged to a cause you support. Your allowance money could be given toward environmental efforts, cancer research, or a community project in which you believe. The lessons you will learn now will also be an example to your friends, but it is you who will gain most from the volunteer habits you are developing. These are the habits that will enrich your life in the years ahead.

*Doing a 'good turn' may seem a trivial thing
for us grown-ups, but a good turn
done as a child will grow into service for the
community when she grows up.*

— Lady Baden-Powell Olave

— 61 —

I'm a yuppie with three kids.
What can I do?

You are a part of the most educated group of individuals ever to populate this land. Your generation stands ready to inherit $7 trillion, which is more funds than any generation in history. What are you doing to help improve the world and your family? The most important thing you can do for your family is to volunteer in your community; be a role model, a person who gives.

Children of all ages need to understand what love looks like. It is up to you to show them. As a parent you show your children love by enabling them to step out into the world on their own. Loving your children is telling them the truth about life, starting with the truth about the needs of others in your own neighborhood. As they become more mature in their abilities to understand, it will be time for them to learn the truth about the needs of others throughout the world. The more they understand the truth about what is really going on in the world from you, as a volunteer, the more they will be able to face the truth of the world ahead for them! And the truth will certainly set them free.

How can we expect our children
to know and experience the joy of giving
unless we teach them that the greater
pleasure in life lies in the art of giving
rather than receiving.

— JAMES CASH PENNY

I'm a Brownie Girl Scout. What can I do?

You are the future of the world. The Brownie Girl Scout promise is, "On my honor, I will try to help God and my country, to help people at all times, and to live by the Girl Scout Law." This oath represents the very meaning of voluntarism by saying you will try your best to help make a difference in the world.

Since you are a Brownie Girl Scout you're probably not even ten years old, and this is a wonderful time for you! You can learn how to practice your Brownie promise at home by helping your parents when they ask — and even when they don't. You can also be a better Brownie by learning that there are many people who are not as fortunate as you and that they need your help.

Now is the time for you to learn how to volunteer, so that when you grow up you will understand that helping people who are not as lucky as you will make you feel better as well as them. The people who lead your Brownie Scout troop are volunteers who help you get your badges and assist with your projects. Someday maybe you will have a little girl in Brownie Girl Scouts and you can be her volunteer troop leader. Until then, let me promise you that the most fun you will ever have is when you take time to make someone else happy. That is really what being a Brownie Scout is all about.

Youth expects fun in the getting,
age reflects on the fun
of having given.

— Milton Murray

How can I encourage others to volunteer?

You teach voluntarism only by example. Volunteering in your community is a strong and powerful message to the people you know. As you spend time with your friends, it is certainly your civic responsibility to ask them if they will participate in activities or projects that match their abilities to give. If your friends decline your requests to participate in your charity, you must accept their answer and let them know how important your own involvement is to you.

As time passes, your friends will see the benefits of voluntarism in your life. You will speak volumes about your character when you spend time giving from your heart. All the world loves a winner. The winners of the world are those who have faced life and determined that giving is more important than receiving. That is a position your friends will first admire and then want to join.

Whether or not your friends and associates decide to find meaning in your acts of volunteering is up to them, but let them have the choice of following your example and becoming a giver for life, just like you. You might just be surprised by their response.

Whatever good there is in the world
I inherit from the courage and work
of those who went before me.
I, in turn, have a responsibility
to make things better for those
who will inherit the world from me.

-— Arthur Dobrin

What can volunteering do for my marriage?

Volunteering as a married couple fortifies, enriches, and enlarges your individual capacities for giving. Love is action — not words. Love is expansive — not limited. A couple who shows their love by giving to others is twice blessed in their love for each other.

If you want to learn to love deeply, allow your love to radiate to all who know you. If you love selectively, you are always at risk of losing the target of your affection and attention. Volunteering gives you and your spouse countless opportunities for selfless connections that demonstrate your capacity for allowing love to flow through both of you to others. Marriage is a sacred opportunity for you each to become givers to each other, to your community, and to the world.

You will see miracles in your marriage when you volunteer together. How could your marriage not be enriched by witnessing the joy on the face of your beloved when you see him or her give from his or her heart to make a difference in the world? Your marriage will be the recipient of that joy and happiness. You will experience more love in your home as you give your love to others.

As a couple loves others, they will find how to better love each other. Volunteering is a loving act that may be one of the true secrets of a lasting marriage.

Don't talk of love, show me!

— Miss Eliza Doolittle in *My Fair Lady*

— 65 —

What can volunteering do for me as a parent?

When a child sees his or her parents volunteering in their community, it instills a sense of trust as the child sees them taking responsibility to improve the world. Being the role model of a charitable spirit also teaches a child the joy and sense of fulfillment that giving brings. Volunteering is a spiritual value that can be taught to children of any age; it will create happier, healthier adolescents who possess a higher degree of direction and self-confidence.

The parent who is the example, the role model, gets more out of volunteering than does the child. The parent who volunteers not only gets the satisfaction and joy out of helping others now, but also gets the ultimate blessing of knowing that he or she has laid the foundation upon which his or her child can build a good life. There is no better dramatic role for any human to play than the character who influences the lives of children for good.

I think that the most significant work
we ever do, in our whole world,
in our whole life, is done within the four walls
of our own home. All mothers and fathers,
whatever their stations in life,
can make the most significant of contributions
by imprinting the spirit of service
on the souls of their children,
so that the children grow up committed to
making a difference.

— Stephen R. Covey

Can I volunteer my time successfully with a person of another race?

"E Pluribus Unum" means "Out of Many, One" and it is clearly printed on all American coins. Volunteering offers you the opportunity to look into the eyes of another human being without seeing his or her race, color, creed, or nationality. America's culture is rapidly changing and we should all prepare for the future. For example, the Asian-American population is expected to triple by the mid-twenty-first century and is predicted that one in five Americans will be Hispanic in fifty years.

This country has become the largest cultural melting pot in the world. In 1997 there were 194.5 million white Americans, 32.2 million African-Americans, 29.2 million Hispanics, 9.5 million Asians, and 2 million American Indians. The culture of America's melting pot offers far more diversity than it did in 1950 when the population was virtually half of what it is today. You are challenged to join others in finding the solution to bringing people together.

The Peace Corps and other international volunteer agencies stress the importance of voluntarism around the world with people of every race as a tool to help promote a better understanding of cultural differences. The Peace Corps could be an opportunity for you to meet people of varying races, colors, and religions. A world of new volunteer opportunities also awaits you with Catholic Relief Service, Church World Service, or the Joint Jewish Distribution Committee.

If international voluntarism is too much of a commitment for you, then you can start at home. Would you consider tutoring a child of another race? How about serving food at a homeless shelter that is open to people in need regardless of race? "We are one" in this world. If you have not discovered this profound truth in your own life, then volunteering can be your way to start.

The American people have a genius for splendid and unselfish action, and into the hands of America, God has placed the destinies of afflicted humanity.

— POPE PIUS XII

Can volunteering be a way to meet new and interesting people?

The very nature of volunteering is to be a part of the world of new and interesting people. This altruistic attitude offers you the opportunity to be around other people who are genuinely committed to making a difference in the world.

You must ask yourself the question "What kind of new and interesting people would I like to meet? Where would I find them?" Each agency or organization has a primary function, which makes it an ideal way for you to meet people you find interesting. There are also a variety of volunteer jobs and tasks within each organization. If you want to know the "movers and shakers" in your community, it would be a good idea to spend time on a fund-raising committee to "meet and greet the elite." Should you desire to meet intellectuals in your area, then volunteer at a university or organization of people who gather to resolve issues and problems.

Volunteering opens up for us new doors to exciting opportunities of service and to new and interesting people we would otherwise never have met.

Volunteers... are looking not only for opportunities to satisfy esteem and self-actualization needs, but also for a chance to build relationships and to satisfy love and belonging needs as well.

— G. T. Berns and Man H. Smith

Can volunteering make grandparents feel young again?

Grandparents who volunteer provide love and wisdom so desperately needed in our society. The contributions you as a grandparent make by volunteering will give you a sense of being needed, a heightened sense of self-esteem, and can actually strengthen your immune system for a longer and healthier lifespan.

The Foster Grandparents of America Program (started in 1965) allows low-income seniors over age sixty to develop a relationship with children who have exceptional or special needs. This program is one of the many programs sponsored through the National Senior Citizen Service Corps. It includes over a half-million volunteers age fifty-five and over.

Foster Grandparents' Traveling Grannies is a volunteer agency targeted for senior women to spend five hours a week with young teen mothers who are pregnant. These loving women mentor and guide young mothers regarding the care of their children. There is also another program for Traveling Grandpas who work with teen fathers or teens considered "at risk of becoming a father."

There is so much that can make a volunteer grandparent feel young again. The "Fountain of Youth" has been found. Why are you not taking advantage of it today?

A human being is happiest and most successful when dedicated to a cause outside his own individual, selfish satisfaction.

— BENJAMIN SPOCK

Can volunteering make an old athlete feel young again?

You have been gifted with athletic discipline, strength, and abilities. Your special athletic gifts can be your gift back to the world by working with young people to inspire, direct, and encourage their abilities toward excellence. Volunteering your skills by coaching sports places you face to face with all the drama and emotion that life can offer. Your young athletes will experience defeat, victory, exuberance, despair, and anticipation, and they will turn to you to share their experiences. This level of intimacy will offer you a level of timeless joy that knows no age.

Volunteering engages you in the big game of life. Athletics requires all your finite skills to be fully alive and present for every emotional response, every thought, every nerve response aimed at winning. Your community has much to learn from your athletic training and abilities. There are many teams in your area in desperate need of coaches for soccer, basketball, baseball, and other sports. Call your mayor's office or local volunteer center to find out who to contact in order to use your gifts and feel young again.

There is much more in store for the old athlete than athlete's foot or a large-size tummy. Years of joy await the experienced athletes who give their athletic zeal to young people anxious to pursue the same exhilarating bliss.

When you are laboring for others,
let it be with the same zeal
as if it were for yourself.

— CONFUCIUS

Can volunteering be my way to "Do unto others"?

Yes, Matthew 7:12 tells us, "Whatsoever you wish that men would do to you, do so to them." The Talmud teaches, "What is hateful to you, do not to your fellow men. That is the entire law, all the rest is commentary." If the entire world practiced this simple lesson, it would be filled with happy people.

You have a chance to change the world by practicing the Golden Rule in your own life. Make it your personal goal to treat those in your community with respect and love. Seek opportunities to help others when you can. Use the skills and talents given to you, and give them back by voluntarily helping others.

It is in giving that we receive. Rewards for your generosity will come in unexpected moments and fill your heart with treasures you have never dreamed possible. By being a volunteer you will live a longer and healthier life and have a higher sense of appreciation and acceptance of others and a greater clarity about the meaning and purpose of life.

"As we do to others, they will do to us." That is the volunteer's way of stating the Golden Rule.

Voluntarism flourishes in a free society among individuals who live by the Golden Rule, yet see the need for self-actualization.

— MARY LAWRENCE

How do I deal with fellow volunteers who are difficult?

Nonprofit voluntarism is a microcosm of all business. You will encounter as you mix and mingle in your community as a volunteer all facets of the human race, ranging from spirit-filled positive persons to spiteful individuals with negative attitudes. You will learn to cut a lot of slack for some of your associates and build friendships with the rest. However, there is an exception. If there is a sour apple in the volunteer barrel who reduces the effectiveness of your agency, go directly to your volunteer coordinator and explain the circumstances. At this point, hopefully, the coordinator will speak to the person and address the issue creating the problem. If the agency does not correct the problem, move on. Your positive volunteering will be put to good use by another nonprofit agency.

Voluntarism is the opportunity for you to use the best of your talents, skills, and energy for the greatest good of the cause. It is not meant to be a breeding ground for personality conflicts or dissension on any level that could harm you or the direction or reputation of the charity. Every volunteer must rely on the agency for their structure, procedure, and rules of operation so he or she may contribute successfully. The agency should be notified if problems need to be brought to their attention. If things are not corrected, change agencies.

There is always going to be someone who is difficult in your life, and there are no exceptions in the world of voluntarism. How you deal with difficult people is the true test of you as person. My suggestion is simply this — treat all difficult volunteers with understanding and love. Look for the good they do, not for the difficulties they create. When you can no longer do this, then just move on. There is another volunteer job awaiting you where beauty and truth — not difficulty — reside. But if you can stay just a little longer you may be able to work out the problems with the difficult person. Try listening to their point of view before you present yours. Put your feet in their shoes and try to follow Richard Carlson's suggestion — "don't sweat the small stuff."

Love the beautiful, seek out the true.
Wish for the good, and the best do.

— Moses Mendelssohn

How can I deal with friends who refuse to volunteer for a charity I support?

The finest example you can set for your friends is your personal witness to the law of giving and receiving. You will teach your friends your own commitment by setting an example as an understanding giver. Be a loving example and your friends will respect you for the courage of your convictions. I believe the next time you approach your friends with a request for their support, they just might be more prone to say yes.

Many of your friends have been desensitized to human need and suffering as they sit in their easy chairs with the remote control in their hands. They have become numb to the images on their television screens of famine, war, domestic violence, and homelessness. They may say to themselves, "What can I do? The world is mayhem and I'm just one person." Your answer to them is "You are missing the point. Making a difference in the world is up to you." But they will only see this if they first observe it in your life. You are making a difference as a volunteer and this just might be the message that wakes them up.

It is not fair to ask others
what you are not willing
to do yourself.

— ELEANOR ROOSEVELT

In my last volunteer job, they didn't thank me. Am I being too sensitive?

No, you are not being too sensitive. Most people, like you, volunteer because they believe in the cause they have chosen to support and appreciate the fact that the agency provides the structure for their volunteer job. They realize they aren't volunteering for praise, awards, or applause from their agency but still believe the agency should be sensitive enough to recognize their efforts.

There is generally a joyful community among volunteers, who express their gratitude to each another as they serve side-by-side. On your next volunteer job you might just want to make it your responsibility to stress gratitude with your team members and let them know they are appreciated for their time and efforts. It only takes a smile and a kind word to brighten someone's day.

Gratitude is one of the strongest of all human emotions. Cicero called it "The mother of all the rest." As volunteers we need to be thanked, but we also must learn to be grateful for the opportunity given us to serve others. After all, the giver always gets back more than the receiver.

Should not the giver be
thankful that the receiver received?
Is not giving a need?
Is not receiving, mercy?

— Friederich W. Nietzsche

Volunteering with Corporations and Charities

If you would like to live in a community
in which you may have pride,
then dedicate yourself in a spirit of humility
to your responsibilities in that community.

— HERBERT VICTOR PROCHNOW

How can I volunteer at work?

Mark Twain said "Happiness is to do what you love and to love what you do." At work, can you say you are really happy? If not, one way to find that missing ingredient in your life could be to volunteer and do something you love.

Approach your supervisor or employer and ask them if your company has a relationship with a local community activity or charity where you could volunteer. If they have not yet selected a public cause to champion, then it may be an ideal opportunity for you to research and find a community need to which you can introduce your company for their support.

By 1990 the National Volunteer Center had organized more than 1,100 United States corporations to develop structured activities that involve their employees in community service. You can volunteer your time or talent in a variety of ways: the "team model" organizes a team of employees who plan and implement group volunteer activities; or under the "volunteer clearinghouse model" which offers choices of volunteer jobs to choose; or your company may refer you to a local volunteer center.

Community partnerships, nonfinancial investments, and profitable social responsibility can offer companies of all sizes new ways to widen their community relationships. And community involvement is definitely good business.

— C. WILLIAM VERITY JR.

Is it good business for a corporation to promote voluntarism?

Sponsoring voluntarism is definitely good for business. As consumers lean toward products and services from companies who support community involvement, companies are making sure their deeds go noticed by their customers. Social responsibility has become big business for corporate America. In fact, in San Francisco an organization of eight-hundred companies calling themselves Business for Social Responsibility has been created.

Reports say that 82 percent of corporations support a variety of sponsored volunteer programs and 26 percent of those corporations give their employees paid time off to allow their participation. A recent Gallup pole found that eight out of ten people said they would do volunteer work if their companies gave them paid time to do it.

Companies that aligned themselves with nonprofit agencies in 1997 spent more than $500 million to sponsor community events or visible social programs. A good example is Starbucks Coffee which donates the profits from the sale of Oprah's Book Club selections at Starbucks to the Starbucks Foundation which supports literacy in local communities. Starbucks also encourages its employees to volunteer their support of literacy efforts through local tutoring and mentoring programs.

He profits most who serves best.

— Arthur F. Sheldon

Can volunteering give me more fulfilling work?

Tired of being in your office all day long? Volunteering can open new professional and social domains and lead you to more fulfilling work. Volunteering to do something you enjoy will add a dimension of passion to your daily life. If your professional life doesn't use all your talents and interests, then volunteering can add spice to your life.

Volunteering can add to your credibility in the community by showcasing your talents. New future professional contacts can result by associating yourself with leaders in various professions who are volunteering. You will have the opportunity to learn more about the key issues in a field that interests you. If you have a flair for organization, fundraising, marketing, or music, a place is waiting for you. Don't forget: new contacts are a two-way street. Volunteer work offers you an exciting new network for personal and professional contacts. A volunteer job puts you in contact with those who can possibly include you in their vocational endeavors. What a bargain! You help others and end up getting assistance in your own personal career path.

In proportion, as one loses himself in [a great cause]... in the same degree does he get the highest happiness out of his work.

— BOOKER T. WASHINGTON

Can volunteering change a company's image?

According to a recent report of two thousand consumers, 76 percent of them will switch brands to stores that seem concerned about their community. This statistic is up 14 percent from three years ago. Companies offering community involvement are capturing the hearts and pocketbooks of local consumers. Corporations are gaining in their awareness that their employee volunteers for charitable groups create rapport with their customers.

More than one hundred large corporations have pledged both volunteer time and money for community support. Kimberly-Clark is spending $2 million and has offered thousands of its employees to participate in the construction of new playgrounds in thirty cities around the country. Noah's New York Bagels opened seventy new stores in 1997 and sent its employees to spend a day together on various community volunteer efforts to paint shelters or crisis centers. Maxwell House Coffee contributed $2 million toward a campaign in 1997 to encourage people to volunteer with Habitat for Humanity in the construction of one hundred new homes for the poor.

It Is amazing to me that any company would fail to see the economic and social power of voluntarism.

Corporations must serve society, even seek out ways to do so.

— ANDREW HEISKELL

How can I volunteer at my church, synagogue, or mosque?

Places of worship rely heavily on volunteer assistance to help their limited staff perform a variety of tasks. Most churches, synagogues, and mosques operate on very limited budgets. People like you are needed to share in the tasks and responsibilities ranging from directing and parking cars during worship services to child care, newsletter publication, prayer groups, hospital sick call visits, and even spring cleaning!

Many years ago I was privileged to be minister of a new church being built from scratch by a young congregation that had little money but lots of dedicated volunteer time. One male parishioner agreed to draw the plans for the new church for free. One female member volunteered to be the church secretary — no charge. Several hundred unskilled members agreed to make one pound chocolate-covered Easter eggs that sold for $1 each, all proceeds going to the building fund. A group of parishioners shivered through several cold Christmas seasons selling Christmas trees to pay for the new wing on the building. The church was built almost totally on volunteer effort. And what a strong church it was!

Call your place of worship today. Offer yourself as a volunteer and experience their effusive gratitude as they gladly accept your offer to volunteer.

Put your hands to work, and your hearts to God.

— Mother Ann Lee

How can I volunteer with youth groups?

There are currently one billion youth between the ages of fifteen and twenty-four on this earth, which makes this the largest generation to ever live at once in the history of the world. They need love and attention. This is a challenge that faces each and every one of us regardless of where we live.

How can we help the youth of the world today? We can start by sharing our individual skills with them. What skills would you like to offer youth groups? If you are a good homemaker, you could work with teenagers who are young parents. If you are a senior citizen who is also a craftsperson by hobby or profession, you can help young people by teaching them carpentry, auto mechanics, gardening, or bricklaying. If you are an artist by hobby or profession, you would be a welcome addition to any school or scout troop.

There is an endless list of youth-related needs within walking distance of your own home. Look within your heart and ask yourself "How can I help?" and then call your local volunteer center, mayor's office or school district office and ask for advice regarding youth groups where you can offer your skills and time. Although the youth group with which you volunteer receives your gifts of love and caring, it is surely you who walks home with a lilt in your step and a whistle on your lips from your encounter with the youth who are the future of this great world in which we all live.

I met an eighty-year-old man who goes to school every day as a volunteer counseling junior high school students. He had been doing it regularly since he retired. I took note of several things about this man for possible application to my life: he constantly smiled and looked twenty years younger. Ah! The true benefits of volunteering.

Youth groups are waiting for you to help them serve the young people in your community today. Don't you wish someone like you had been there when you needed them, when you were young?

***Service to youth is the rent we pay
for the space we occupy on earth.***

— Jane Deeter Rippin

How can I volunteer at a hospital?

Ever thought about selling popcorn to individuals young and old and collecting more than money? I mean receiving such rewards as smiles and hugs and stories of healing and joy. That's what volunteers at the popcorn stand at Harris Methodist Hospital in Fort Worth, Texas, receive every day from the visitors and patients to whom they sell popcorn.

Most hospitals offer a variety of volunteer opportunities from which to choose. Hospital volunteering is an opportunity to lend your hands and heart to assist the hospital's staff in the service of caring for their patients. Call a hospital in your area and speak to the volunteer services department. They can tell you about their volunteer opportunities or they will send you an application with a list of current available volunteer jobs.

Volunteers are needed in various capacities throughout a hospital and the volunteer services department will offer you a detailed description of the jobs that are available.

You may get no more out of volunteering at a hospital than popcorn on your vest, but because it got there by means of a hug, you will go home a happier and healthier person. Isn't that what you really want?

All who are served by the health care institution that receives your thoughtful gift will be blessed in perpetuity because you cared and you shared.

— ARTHUR C. FRANTZREB

How can I volunteer at the university I attended?

Alumni can call for information about volunteer opportunities through the alumni association or the university's development office. Business and liberal arts graduates, law graduates and others can volunteer to become resource persons for student recruitment and fund-raising. You can serve on committees to plan activities for school alumni, serve as a mentor for graduate students, or help students explore career options.

Volunteering your knowledge and passion to your alma mater is a great gift to the college or university and its students. It is your way of "giving back" as an act of gratitude for what your college or university did for you. It is also an ideal way to challenge yourself by working with young enthusiastic students and by becoming an integral part of the ongoing educational process at your college or university.

Education is a lifetime experience. It did not end when you left your alma mater — it only began. Volunteering can be your way to keep that educational experience alive in your life today, tomorrow, forever.

Don't ever dare to take your college as a matter of course — because like freedom and democracy, many people you'll never know anything about have broken their hearts to get it to you.

— ALICE DUER MILLER

How can I volunteer at an arts group?

There is always a need for volunteers in arts groups. It's often sad but true that local arts groups don't have adequate private or public funding to sponsor their work. These groups rely heavily on volunteer efforts to help in every area of production and to help bring the group's purpose to the public's attention.

You may decide you would like to volunteer by helping build stage sets for a theater production; write press releases for an art show; sell tickets for a musical concert; organize venues for local poets to read their work; or organize a bake sale to raise money for a puppet show teaching kids to "Just Say No" to drugs and alcohol. There is virtually no end to the needs in your local arts community.

In New York an anonymous woman volunteers every year to give $25,000 unrestricted grants to each of ten female visual artists, over age thirty, who show creative promise and are at a critical juncture in their careers. To establish these annual grants this marvelous female volunteer has formed the Anonymous Was a Woman Foundation. Three cheers for this woman who is volunteering to help so many visual artists in need. She is truly an inspiration to all of us who could give more to the world of the visual arts.

Are you interested in the performing arts? If so, then call your local theater or dance company. Are you interested in visual art? Call your local museum or art school. Are you interested in music? Call your local symphony, musical group, or high school marching band. There is no end to opportunities for you to volunteer with an arts group. In New Jersey, a shy philanthropist, Raymond G. Chambers, recently gave $12 million as the lead gift for the New Jersey

Performing Arts Center in Newark. After making a fortune several years ago, he retired to spend the rest of his life giving his time and money to others. The performing arts will never be the same in the "Garden State" thanks to this extraordinary volunteer.

Volunteering with arts groups will enliven your world by introducing you to creative and passionate people you otherwise might not meet. These exciting people will become a part of your life and bring to you what the arts are all about — creative channels to life's true meaning.

My heart is ever at your service.

— WILLIAM SHAKESPEARE

— 83 —

How can I volunteer with an international agency?

Short-term international volunteer positions generally last from one week to three months and offer a variety of projects and countries from which to choose. You may want to volunteer for a job involving environmental issues in India, health projects in Zimbabwe, work on a farm in Denmark, or help reconstruct a castle in the Czech Republic. They may require that you pay all your own expenses.

Long-term positions may last from a few months to a lifetime of service, but an average long-term project requires a minimum of a two or three year volunteer commitment. Generally, the charity pays all your expenses for long-term volunteer assignments. The United States government offers the Peace Corps, and the United Nations has a number of volunteer programs. There are also many opportunities available through religious organizations such as Catholic Relief Service, Church World Service, and the Joint Jewish Distribution Committee.

There are more than 250 international agencies offering worldwide volunteer positions. Call your local volunteer agency for information regarding international volunteer assignments. You can be an ambassador of this country and represent the spirit of voluntarism to the world. What are you waiting for?

Each one of us
can work for a small change
in the world around us.

— Lamar S. Smith

— 84 —

How can I volunteer at a social service agency?

Social service agencies are nonprofit organizations whose main goal is to improve the lives of individuals in the community through various assistance programs. Federal funds often subsidize agency programs, and in so doing, offset state or county expenses. Most social service agency financial support, however, comes from voluntary contributions.

Social service agencies include protective services to children and adults, in-home supportive services for the elderly and disabled, foster care and adoption services, family services, homeless shelters, public assistance, and senior citizen programs. Shining examples of social service agencies are the YMCA and YWCA, Salvation Army, American Red Cross, Junior Achievement, Boys and Girls Clubs of America, I Have a Dream, Big Brothers and Big Sisters, and the Boy Scouts/Girl Scouts of America.

Relevant issues of community need can be served through the loving and compassionate volunteers who work with these agencies. Your local yellow pages will give you complete listings of the agencies in your area under the section "social services." Why not let your fingers start walking through the Yellow Pages today?

*Today, I ask all Americans
and all institutions, large and small,
to make service central
to your life and work.*

— GEORGE BUSH

— 85 —

How can I change my volunteering from one charity to another?

Interests change over time, and certain causes are more relevant and pertinent in various stages of your life. Volunteer organizations expect a certain degree of attrition. You would be wise to choose your charity as you would choose a paid job, carefully and with much consideration. Remember, there are hundreds of charities where you can volunteer.

If you feel you could better serve another agency or charity, then let your volunteer coordinator know your intentions as well as the date you will no longer be available to continue the job. This courtesy allows your agency to replace you with another volunteer and gives you an opportunity for a fair closure with them.

If you are dissatisfied with the job at your charity or have questions about their focus or direction, this is certainly the time to air your grievances before you officially resign. The discussion with your volunteer coordinator may involve vital points for your charity to consider regarding their future activities. They would much rather know your reasons for quitting and if possible work out the differences with you than have you withdraw your volunteer support with no known explanation. Changing charities may be best for both you and the organization. Your volunteer work began as a joyful experience — let it end the same way.

The fabric of American life
is woven around our tens of thousands
of voluntary associations.

— Herbert C. Hoover

How can I change my volunteer job?

Changing anything is not an easy task, but in the world of volunteering it may be the most important stimulus for you to continue your interest and commitment.

Your volunteer coordinator wants you to enjoy your job and is willing to help make your job a good experience. Be advised, however, that a paid agency employee will train you for your volunteer job and you training is a time-consuming agency expense, so choose your job carefully!

If you decide to change your job within the agency you serve, ask your agency if they would like for you to train your replacement. This advance warning gives them time to check their available volunteer replacements for your job and to find you a new job in the agency that better suits your time and talents.

Do you want to change your volunteer job? Do it today. It will not only be the best thing you do for yourself, but it will also benefit the charity you have so lovingly served.

Do all the good you can,
By all the means you can,
In all the ways you can,
In all the places you can,
At all the times you can
To all the people you can,
As long as you ever can.

— JOHN WESLEY

Has the Peace Corps really made a difference?

More than 140,000 volunteers have passed through the Peace Corps since 1961 and have gone on to become solid citizens and community activists around the world. In fact, former members of the Peace Corps have become ambassadors, governors, foreign service officers, directors of large national and multinational businesses, bank presidents and owners of small enterprises.

The Peace Corps has taken its volunteers to more than one hundred countries and trained them for assignments in such fields as agriculture, community development, education, business, health/nutrition, and natural resources.

Is the Peace Corps for you? Jimmy Carter's mother thought so: Lilian Carter went to India as a nurse. Small wonder her son has made volunteering with Habitat for Humanity International a vital part of his post-Presidential life. Have the Carters made a difference? Most people would say "yes." A very large part of the credit goes to Mrs. Carter and her years of voluntary service in the Peace Corps.

Throughout my life, I've seen the difference that volunteering efforts can make in people's lives. I know the personal value of service as a local volunteer.

— JIMMY CARTER

Has AmeriCorps really made a difference?

AmeriCorps is making a difference. There are currently over twenty thousand members serving full or part time in more than 350 AmeriCorps programs nationwide. In exchange for volunteer service, members receive education awards. Our nation is privileged to have AmeriCorps members work on various community levels to help plan and implement strategies to strengthen this country.

AmeriCorps members have helped fight illiteracy, tutored at-risk youth, organized neighborhood watch associations, provided assistance to crime victims, and prevented crime through conflict resolution. They assist in building affordable housing, help seniors live independently, immunize children against preventable diseases, clean up city streets, restore national parks, and provide relief to areas hit hard by natural disaster.

Is this for you? Make an inquiry and find out more about AmeriCorps today.

I challenge a new generation of young Americans to a season of service to act on your idealism by helping troubled children, keeping company with those in need, reconnecting our torn communities. There is much to be done — enough indeed for millions of others who are still young in spirit to give themselves in service too.

— BILL CLINTON

Have organizations like
Habitat for Humanity International
really made a difference?

Habitat for Humanity International inspires the spirit of giving and receiving within the heart of every homeowner and volunteer assisting in the construction of a new home for the poor. Habitat for Humanity was founded in 1976 by Millard and Linda Fuller, and 100,000 homes will have been built throughout the world by the year 2000. These homes are not free to their owners. Homeowners are entitled to an interest-free mortgage after they agree to make monthly payments on the house, and devote hours of "sweat equity" by working on their home, and the homes of others. An average house is about 1,000 square feet in size and the home values are determined by the price of the land and the outstanding costs of the materials for construction. The labor to build the house is donated primarily by volunteers.

Habitat for Humanity International extends their volunteering services beyond just helping to build houses. They assign volunteers to stay close to the families living in their new homes for at least a year or more. This ongoing commitment between the homeowner and volunteers helps to build strong bonds between people by weaving the rich texture of community and good citizenship.

In Oprah Winfrey's national volunteer program "Oprah's Angel Network" she has encouraged individuals throughout the country to donate time and money directly to Habitat for Humanity to help build homes for the needy. Oprah has personally pledged to raise millions of dollars to build Habitat homes in 205 cities throughout the United States.

"Does Habitat for Humanity work?" The answer is "You bet it does!" Its focus is one that more charities need to adopt which is to help others to help themselves. Millard and Linda Fuller have a single goal that every person on this planet will have a simple decent place in which to live. The hundreds of thousands of Habitat volunteers through the world are beginning to make this dream come true. Don't you want to join them as a Habitat volunteer today?

The highest service we can perform
for others is to help them
help themselves.

— Horace Mann

Has the International Red Cross really made a difference?

The International Red Cross had its beginnings in 1859. Austrian and French armies fought in Solferino, a town in northern Italy, and after sixteen hours of fighting there were forty-thousand dead and wounded soldiers left on the battlefield to die. On the evening of this battle, a Swiss citizen named Henry Durant passed through that area on business and found these forty-thousand men lying in a field with no medical attention. The tragedy so appalled him that he wrote a book called A Memory of Solferino which he self-published and circulated among powerful people of the time. The premise of his book was presented and a committee was formed called the International Committee for Relief to the Wounded in the Time of War, which later became the International Red Cross.

Today the International Red Cross is the largest volunteer agency in the world. There is not an hour of any day that the Red Cross is not rendering service somewhere in the world. If you have wondered where to start as a volunteer, you cannot go wrong by considering the Red Cross. It has meant a lot to others — it can be the volunteer opportunity that will change your life today.

I would rather have originated
the Red Cross than to have written
the Constitution of the United States.

— WILL ROGERS

Can I really trust the charity where I volunteer?

In almost every case the answer is "Yes." Nonprofit agencies are held to state and national standards of accountability. If you have any questions about your charity, you may contact the National Charities Information Bureau in New York City or the Philanthropic Advisory Service (which is a division of the Better Business Bureau). The Better Business Bureau has set standards to promote ethical practices by nonprofit agencies in order to inspire public confidence and encourage the growth of community voluntarism and contributions. You may receive a copy of their standards by calling your local bureau.

Ask your charity for its mission statement regarding the history, purpose, and activities of the agency. If you have questions regarding their financial accountability, don't be afraid to ask for their annual report and a copy of their Internal Revenue Service Form 990 (a financial form including detailed information on a charity's income and expenses, which must be filed annually). If you still have questions, you should contact your state's attorney general's office for further information. Most charities can be trusted. Check them out and you will find out for yourself.

The genius of the tradition as it has developed in America is the unique combination of giving and voluntary service on behalf of independent organizations and institutions devoted to the public interest.

— Robert L. Payton

Are corporations and charities supporting the Presidents' Summit for America's Future?

America's Promise–The Alliance For Youth has summoned all Americans to help find ways to provide today's children and youth with safe places to play and learn, a marketable skill, and an opportunity to serve the community. The goal is to reach two million youth by the end of the year 2000.

The YMCA is providing safe places for children and youth to come together with caring adults in more than 2,000 YMCAs across the country. Over the next three years the YMCA has also committed to recruiting an additional 190,500 volunteers for a total of 572,000 volunteers to help teach children the values of caring, honesty, respect, and responsibility.

AT&T has committed $150 million, making this one of the single largest contributions ever made to education. It has agreed to connect America's 110,000 public and private elementary and secondary schools to the Information Superhighway by the year 2000.

It is good business to be a champion of voluntarism. The 1997 Presidents' Summit for America's Future led by General Colin Powell made this a cornerstone of corporate America's future. Corporations and charities are responding to General Powell's challenge. For more information call 1-888-555-Youth or, fax (703)884-7388, or visit the Website (www.americapromise.org).

Will America's corporations and charities really make a difference by responding positively to General Powell's call to action? I say, yes! We have to start realizing that solving the problems of at-risk youth is dependent upon more than just our governmental agencies. It involves each of us as we volunteer our time, talent and treasure at our corporation or favorite charity. The problems are big, but we as volunteers are bigger. America's youth can be reached, but it starts with you and me.

My hope is to have every corporation and organization in our country modify its mission to include some level of participation in our partnership.

— GENERAL COLIN POWELL

— 93 —

Can volunteering prepare me for a nonprofit vocation?

Yes, volunteering is an opportunity for you to glimpse the inner workings of the nonprofit world and consider whether your volunteer avocation might become a paying vocation. Women are often introduced to social service agencies, charities, and causes when their children are still in school and they aren't working outside the home. These women often connect with the fundamental principles and attitudes involved in efforts aimed at supporting community need and change. It is often a natural transition for dedicated volunteers to seek paid, full-time employment in the field of nonprofit organizations after being involved with a community service agency.

Educated and trained professionals generally manage a nonprofit agency and oversee the training of volunteers to teach them skills necessary to promote the mission of the charity. Training programs present opportunities for you to ask pertinent questions about job possibilities with the agency. These learning situations often prepare volunteers like you for rewarding employment opportunities.

Where do you learn the skills for your vocation? Sometimes in a school, oft-times in life's experiences, but many times in your volunteer job.

Employment is nature's physician, and is essential to human happiness.

— GALEN (129–199 A.D.)

Section V

Volunteering around the World

*The world cannot always understand
one's profession of faith,
but it can understand service.*

— Ian MacLaren

Doesn't the government already do what I'll be asked to do as a volunteer?

Government alone is not capable of dealing with the many social needs in today's world. The challenge for government today is to help share the responsibility by changing the culture of the nation and to help in institutionalizing voluntarism as a corporate and personal responsibility to make this world a better place in which to live.

John F. Kennedy asked us to consider "...not what your country can do for you, but what you can do for your country." That is the true call of voluntarism. That is the challenge to do what government cannot do for itself. It is also what has kept us strong and effective as a nation.

Volunteer and governmental agencies will succeed as partners with far less money than the government would spend on its own. Some say a nonprofit agency can successfully do with one dollar what the government does with ten. While this could be an exaggeration, perhaps the time has come for more partnerships between the public and private sectors to solve more of this nation's social issues. Why not join that partnership as a volunteer today?

No matter how big and powerful government gets, and the many services it provides, it can never take the place of volunteers.

— RONALD REAGAN

Can volunteering affect major world problems?

Mother Teresa proved over and over again with her small group of nuns that seemingly desperate causes could be handled through small but consistent volunteer efforts. World change actually begins when small clusters of people stand up and insist on finding a solution to a problem. The average volunteer spends four hours a week volunteering within six miles of his or her own home. Grass-roots movements have stood the test of time as communities gather to deal with a variety of local issues, such as high rates of illiteracy, teen pregnancy, and education. Massive corps of volunteers have united to address major problems that affect the entire world.

During times of world crisis neighborhood churches and agencies often gather blankets, coats, and canned goods to send overseas. Local citizens organize toy drives for children's hospitals to ship to areas of war or famine. The undaunted human spirit unites all of us, in love, to change the world.

Giant industries are also stepping forward to offer skilled volunteers for effecting world change. LensCrafters has promised to provide free eye care for one million needy people around the world (especially children); Big Brothers and Big Sisters plans to double its number of mentors to 200,000; Girl Scouts will dedicate 8.5 million hours of community service to mark its eighty-fifth anniversary. By the year 2000 hundreds of corporations, churches and social organizations will be donating millions of hours of time in a partnership of all Americans led by General Colin Powell.

When the devastating earthquake hit Mexico City several years ago, the government was of limited help in the early hours of need. But help was there, and it came from the volunteer efforts of nonprofit organizations throughout the world which were ready to be of assistance immediately.

The world is like a mirror;
frown at it, and it frowns on you.
Smile, and it smiles, too.

— HERBERT SAMUEL

Is volunteering a way to bring peace to the world?

It is by opening our hearts and giving love that the world will find peace. It is the legacy left by Princess Diana, Mother Teresa, Gandhi, and so many more.

Fourteen million children die throughout the world each year due to starvation. You may not have global power and contacts to change this sad fact, but can you help feed one hungry child in your city? Peace begins with one person, and the person it starts with is you.

You are given a clear choice every day to offer your time, talent, and treasure to a cause that will make a difference in someone's life. If you choose to give rather than take, you are on your way to helping bring peace into this troubled world. You can't help everyone, but you can change the life of someone. That changed life brings us all one step closer to peace.

Think about it. You take the time to mentor one "throwaway" at-risk youngster in your community and you make it possible for him or her to have a chance to live a normal life rather than one of poverty and crime. Does that one saved life change the whole world and bring us peace? Maybe not — but it does bring us one life closer to that goal.

Peace we want because
there is another war to fight;
against poverty and disease.

— INDIRA GANDHI

Is volunteering catching on in other countries?

World leaders are addressing the challenges of literacy; coeducational training in the fields of industry and agriculture; equal access to education; employment opportunities; eligibility to vote; the value of women in and out of the home; health care; aging and the elderly; disabled persons; prevention of crime and convict rehabilitation; control of illegal drugs; assistance to children; and help with natural disasters, starvation, civil strife, and epidemics.

Many volunteer programs offer international volunteer opportunities. Doctors Without Borders volunteers physicians and nurses from around the world to countries requiring medical attention due to war, civil strife, epidemics or natural disasters. Each year more than 2,000 health-care workers volunteer their time from forty-five nations in more than seventy countries. The Peace Corps sends 6,500 volunteers to more than ninety-three countries. The United Nations hosts more than 2,000 volunteers from over one hundred countries. The International Red Cross has volunteers from many countries serving locally and internationally wherever there is a need. Volunteering is catching on in other countries around the world. This may well be the new foundation for lasting peace for which we have been hoping.

One more good man on earth
is better than an extra angel
in heaven.

— CHINESE PROVERB

Can volunteering make my neighborhood more beautiful?

Ask the volunteers from Austin, Texas, if volunteering three hours one Saturday morning made their neighborhood more beautiful. In April 1996, from nine until noon that same day, 3,170 volunteers collected 550,000 pounds of litter as part of their Keep Austin Beautiful Operation. This cleanup program not only beautified their neighborhoods, but saved taxpayers approximately $880,000.

On Earth Day in April 1997, Orange County in Southern California, organized a coastal cleanup; in a two-weekend festival atmosphere there were opportunities for cleanup as well as educational hikes, an insect and reptile show, talent shows, games, garden shows, and tables of food! In the midst of their educational and entertaining weekend, the volunteers pulled weeds, planted trees, and picked up litter.

Small neighborhood volunteer cleanups are also successful. Print flyers and leave them in your neighbors' mailboxes within a two or three-block radius. Tell your neighbors to bring their own rubber gloves, plastic bags, rakes, and good intentions. You will make new friends and your neighborhood will become a more beautiful place in which to live.

Each citizen should play his
part in the community
according to his individual gifts.

— Plato

Is volunteering a way to keep America strong?

Almost one-third of all Americans volunteer their time, talent, and treasure to keep America strong. Government alone cannot handle vital social issues. It is in the villages and towns that Americans show a commitment to their country by teaching literacy, organizing neighborhood cleanups, offering love and help to disadvantaged youth. These volunteers are the heart, hands and feet of all great patriots who have gone before to make this country strong.

The fiber that weaves the tapestry that is America — blending all races, creeds, and colors — is the spirit of voluntarism. Communities that work and volunteer together have much greater strength to face the challenges of modern life. The injustices in our society motivate us to action and do not discourage the average citizen from taking an active moral stand — volunteering is a way to fight back and to ensure equality of opportunity for all.

If there is a need in your community, find a way to offer yourself to help. Only you can deeply appreciate the issues facing this country and only you can volunteer to roll up your sleeves to help. As long as there is a glimmer of hope, the people of this great nation will find solutions.

Giving and Sharing — An American Tradition.

— U.S. Postage Stamp

Can volunteering help solve the environmental problems around the world?

Volunteers have stepped forward in worldwide cooperation with scientists to work together on projects that benefit the environment. The need for volunteers both nationally and internationally is vital for the health of our planet. Our consumer- oriented throwaway society requires massive cultural education to enact the necessary changes needed for the health of our ecological system.

Many nonprofit groups offer structures for volunteers to participate in environmental change. For example, last year eighty-five thousand volunteers came from every state and nearly every country in the world to donate more than three million hours of service to America's National Park Service.

Projects that relate to the natural environment range from marine ecology, nature conservation, endangered species, air pollution, recycling, water supplies, agricultural issues, and environmental education. Volunteers may choose assignments that deal with any area that they feel strongly about whether local or international. The earth's resources are certainly fragile and require the voluntary cooperation of every person in the world to accomplish the great tasks at hand in the future. Don't you want to be one of these "volunteers for the planet"?

Give a gift to all generations by saving the earth.

— Christina R. Newman

How can we teach volunteering to future generations?

You can only teach what you know. It is timely and imperative that we teach solid and tangible social values to future generations. It is up to you to take the hand of someone you love and show her or him the value of giving. Today there are more young people living on this planet than at any time in history. It is our social and moral responsibility to teach them the solid values gained from civic involvement through voluntarism.

President Bill Clinton expressed his sentiments regarding voluntarism when he said, "Much of the work of America cannot be done by government. The solution must be the American people through voluntary service to others." Clinton went on to say, "...the era of big government may be over but the era of big challenges for our nation is surely not. Our mission is nothing less than to spark a renewed national sense of obligation, a new sense of duty, a new season of service."

We can teach volunteering to future generations, but we will do so only by example. Young people watch, they do not listen. Every day some young person is observing quietly what you are doing as a volunteer. That is all the instruction they need. They just hunger for more of your example.

Nothing is so contagious as example;
and we never do any great good or evil
which does not produce its like.

— Francois de La Rochefoucauld

About the Author

Dr. Douglas M. Lawson is the author of the award-winning bestseller *GIVE TO LIVE: How Giving Can Change Your Life* (Alti Publishing, 1991) currently in it's sixth printing and in three foreign language editions: Spanish, Italian and German, and *GIVE TO LIVE: A Stewardship and Development Program for Your Church*, (Abingdon Press, 1995). He has written numerous articles for such national publications as *Fund Raising Management*, *U.S. Air*, *Southern Bride*, and *Servant Leadership*. He has been the publisher of a monthly newsletter; *Philanthropic Trends Digest*, and eight editions of *The Foundation 500*. Dr. Lawson has produced numerous audio and videotapes, including, *The Artful Asker*, *Give to Live*, and *A Basic Fund-Raiser Course*.

Dr. Lawson holds three academic degrees: a B.A. from Randolph Macon College, a B.D. from Drew University, and a Ph.D. from Duke University. He is a member of three honorary fraternities: Phi Beta Kappa, Omicron Delta Kappa and Pi Gamma Mu. He is a member of the board of directors of Fleetwood Enterprises, a New York Stock Exchange corporation, and he is on the advisory board of the Yale Divinity School, the board of the Houston Junior Achievement, and the American Leprosy Missions board. He has served as a member of the Charitable Giving Task Force of the Million Dollar Round Table.

In his professional life, Dr. Lawson serves as the founding chairman of Douglas M. Lawson Associates, Inc., a fund-raising and management consulting firm which, to date, has served more than one thousand clients throughout the world and assisted clients in raising more than $2 billion. Dr. Lawson is a frequent speaker and lecturer throughout the United States, Mexico, and Canada.

Douglas M. Lawson Associates, Inc., has represented such clients as chapters of the American Red Cross, Habitat for Humanity International, Special Olympics International, Junior

Achievement, C.A.R.E., United States Committee for UNICEF, Girl Scouts of America, and the Robert Schuller Ministries.

For more information on the services of Douglas M. Lawson Associates, Inc., or the availability of Dr. Lawson for speaking engagements, please contact us any time, twenty-four hours a day:

Dr. Douglas M. Lawson
Douglas M. Lawson Associates, Inc.
545 Madison Ave.
New York, New York 10022

Voice: (800)238-0004
fax: (212)759-1893
E-mail: doug@douglawson.com
Home page: www.douglawson.com

To Benefit Society

ALTI Publishing specializes in tailor-made books that support the missions of nonprofit organizations. We are seeking additional book concepts which will help improve the human condition and assist worthy causes.

ALTI assumes the financial risks and contributes a significant portion of the proceeds to charity in addition to standard royalties for the author.

For example, 20% of ALTI's receipts from *VOLUNTEERING: 101 Ways You Can Improve the World and Your Life* is being contributed to nonprofit organizations. Contact us at the address below to learn how your organization may benefit from this donation.

Another of our books, *FROM GRANDMA WITH LOVE, A Legacy of Values*, is benefiting at-risk children by supporting a pledge made to General Colin Powell's America's Promise–The Alliance For Youth organization by the National Head Start Association, Foster Grandparents of America, and the Retired Senior Volunteer Program.

If you have an idea for a great book, we would like to speak with you. The project may be in manuscript form, merely an idea, or somewhere in between. The topic may be either linked directly to the mission of a specific nonprofit organization or a general subject with broad application.

ALTI Publishing
P.O. Box 28025
San Diego, CA 92198
Phone: (800) 284-8537
Fax: (619) 485-9878
E-mail: whilbig@altipublishing.com

To purchase additional copies of this book,
contact your local bookstore
or telephone ALTI Publishing
toll-free at (800) 284-8537.

Just Announced!

THIS NEW POSTAGE STAMP debuts in October 1998 to honor the American tradition of giving and sharing. It is a beautiful, generic stamp for philanthropy. The bee and flower represent the symbiotic relationship between the giver and the recipient. Go to your local post office and — *ask for it* — *use it* — *share it.*

Stamp Design © 1998 U.S. Postal Service. Reproduced with permission.